Learn R for Data Science and Machine Learning

Build Data Models, Visualizations, and Analytics with R

Greyson Chesterfield

COPYRIGHT

DISCLAIMER

The information provided in this book is for general informational purposes only. All content in this book reflects the author's views and is based on their research, knowledge, and experiences. The author and publisher make no representations or warranties of any kind concerning the completeness, accuracy, reliability, suitability, or availability of the information contained herein.

This book is not intended to be a substitute for professional advice, diagnosis, or treatment. Readers should seek professional advice for any specific concerns or conditions. The author and publisher disclaim any liability or responsibility for any direct, indirect, incidental, or consequential loss or damage arising from the use of the information contained in this book.

Contents

Chapter 1: Introduction to R and RStudio

Overview of R Programming for Data Science and Machine Learning

What is R?

R is a powerful and flexible programming language and environment used extensively for statistical computing, data analysis, and graphical representation. It was created by Ross Ihaka and Robert Gentleman at the University of Auckland, New Zealand, in the early 1990s, and has since become one of the most widely-used languages for data science, statistics, and machine learning. R provides a wide array of packages and libraries that make it easy to conduct data analysis and model development.

Unlike other general-purpose programming languages like Python or Java, R is specifically designed for statistical computing and data manipulation. It has a large ecosystem of statistical tools, advanced visualization techniques, and machine learning algorithms, making it the go-to tool for statisticians and data scientists.

Why Use R for Data Science and Machine Learning?

Several key reasons make R an ideal choice for data science and machine learning:

1. **Extensive Libraries and Packages**: R boasts a rich ecosystem of packages and libraries. Libraries such as dplyr, ggplot2, caret, randomForest, and tidyverse provide robust tools for data manipulation, visualization, and machine learning.

2. **Statistical Analysis**: R was built with statistical analysis in mind. It includes built-in functions for a wide range of statistical tests and models, making it particularly valuable for data scientists and researchers who need to perform rigorous statistical analysis.

3. **Visualization**: R has unparalleled capabilities for visualizing data. The ggplot2 library, in particular, provides an intuitive and powerful way to create highly customizable plots that help in understanding data and presenting findings clearly.

4. **Community and Support**: R has a large and active community. From online forums to comprehensive documentation, there are plenty of resources available to help troubleshoot issues and learn new techniques.

5. **Reproducibility**: R encourages reproducible research. It integrates well with R Markdown,

enabling users to create dynamic reports with embedded code and visualizations, which is essential for transparent and reproducible data analysis.

6. **Integration with Other Tools**: R can easily integrate with other tools and languages. For example, R can interface with databases like SQL, web scraping tools like rvest, and big data technologies like Spark using the sparklyr package.

R and Machine Learning

In addition to its strengths in statistical analysis and data manipulation, R has powerful machine learning capabilities. The caret (Classification And REgression Training) package is one of the most popular tools in R for building machine learning models. It provides a consistent interface for training, tuning, and evaluating models, making it easier for users to apply machine learning algorithms without needing to understand the intricacies of each algorithm.

R also supports deep learning through packages like keras, which provides an R interface to the popular Python-based deep learning library. This enables R users to build and train neural networks for tasks such as image classification, time series forecasting, and natural language processing (NLP).

In summary, R is a versatile and powerful language for data science and machine learning. Whether you're a statistician, data analyst, or machine learning engineer, R offers the tools and libraries necessary to carry out complex data analysis tasks, build robust models, and visualize data in meaningful ways.

Installation and Setup of R and RStudio

Before diving into the coding aspect of R, it's essential to get your development environment set up. RStudio is the most popular integrated development environment (IDE) for R, offering a user-friendly interface to work with R. Let's break down the process of installing both R and RStudio.

Installing R

R can be installed on Windows, Mac, and Linux operating systems. The installation process is straightforward.

1. **Download R**:
   - Go to the official R project website: https://cran.r-project.org.
   - Choose the appropriate version for your operating system (Windows, macOS, or Linux).
   - Click the download link for your operating system.

2. **Install R**:
   - After downloading the installation file, run it and follow the prompts.

- For Windows, the default options should be fine for most users. You can leave the default installation directory and choose additional components like Rtools if needed (Rtools is required for compiling packages from source on Windows).

- On macOS and Linux, the installer will guide you through the setup process.

3. **Verify Installation**:

- Once installed, you can verify that R is working by opening the R console. On Windows, you can access R from the Start menu. On macOS, you can find R in the Applications folder.

- Type version into the R console and press Enter. This will display the version of R you have installed, confirming that R is properly installed.

Installing RStudio

RStudio is a free, open-source IDE that provides a rich environment for coding, debugging, and visualizing in R. It makes writing and running R code much more efficient.

1. **Download RStudio**:

- Visit the RStudio website: https://posit.co/download/rstudio-desktop/.

- Choose the free version (RStudio Desktop Open Source License) and download the appropriate installer for your operating system.

2. **Install RStudio**:

   - Run the downloaded file and follow the installation instructions.

   - RStudio will automatically detect your R installation, so you don't need to install RStudio separately.

3. **Launch RStudio**:

   - Once installed, launch RStudio. It should open up with the default R console, which allows you to type and execute R commands interactively.

RStudio Interface Overview

RStudio provides a highly productive and intuitive interface for working with R. Let's go over the key components of the RStudio IDE.

1. **Console**:

   - The console is where you can type and execute R commands interactively. You can also view the results of your code here.

2. **Source**:

   - The source pane is where you can write, edit, and save your R scripts. You can write multiple lines of code here, and then run them in the console.

3. **Environment**:
   - This pane displays a list of variables, functions, and datasets that you have loaded into your R session. You can use this to keep track of your workspace.

4. **History**:
   - This pane shows a history of the commands you've executed in the console. It's helpful if you want to review or re-run previous commands.

5. **Files, Plots, Packages, and Help**:
   - The **Files** tab allows you to navigate your file system to access and open R scripts or data files.
   - The **Plots** tab displays any graphical output generated by your R code.
   - The **Packages** tab allows you to manage and install R packages.
   - The **Help** tab provides quick access to R's documentation and help files.

Basic Syntax in R

Variables and Data Types

In R, you can assign values to variables using the assignment operator <- (or =). Here's an example:

r

```
x <- 5

name <- "Alice"
```

In this example, we assigned the value 5 to the variable x, and the string "Alice" to the variable name.

Vectors

A vector is a basic data structure in R. It is a sequence of data elements of the same type. You can create a vector using the c() function:

r

```
numbers <- c(1, 2, 3, 4, 5)

names <- c("Alice", "Bob", "Charlie")
```

Data Frames

A data frame is similar to a table or a spreadsheet, where each column can hold different types of data. To create a simple data frame:

r

```
df <- data.frame(Name = c("Alice", "Bob", "Charlie"),

                 Age = c(25, 30, 35),
```

Occupation = c("Data Scientist",
"Engineer", "Doctor"))

Functions

In R, functions are defined using the function()
keyword. Here's an example of a basic function:

r

```r
add_numbers <- function(a, b) {

  return(a + b)

}
```

You can then call the function as follows:

r

```r
result <- add_numbers(5, 10)
```

Control Structures

R supports common control structures like loops and
conditionals. For example, here's an if statement:

r

```r
x <- 10
if (x > 5) {

  print("x is greater than 5")
} else {
```

```
  print("x is less than or equal to 5")

}
```

Importing and Exporting Data

To import data from a CSV file into R, you can use the read.csv() function:

r

```
data <- read.csv("path/to/your/data.csv")
```

To export data to a CSV file, use the write.csv() function:

r

```
write.csv(data, "path/to/save/data.csv")
```

Real-World Example: Installing Necessary Packages for Data Analysis

One of the first steps in data analysis with R is installing and loading the necessary libraries. The most commonly used libraries for data analysis are tidyverse, dplyr, ggplot2, and caret. To install a package, use the install.packages() function:

r

```r
install.packages("tidyverse")
```

```r
install.packages("caret")
```

After installation, load the library into your R session using library():

```r
r
```

```r
library(tidyverse)
```

```r
library(caret)
```

These libraries provide a wide range of tools for data manipulation, visualization, and machine learning.

In this chapter, we introduced you to R and RStudio, two essential tools for data science and machine learning. We covered the process of installing R and RStudio, navigating the RStudio interface, and using basic R syntax. We also walked through how to install and load the necessary packages to begin data analysis in R.

Now that you've set up your environment and understood the basics, you're ready to start diving deeper into data science and machine learning with R. In the next chapter, we'll explore data types and structures in R in more detail, providing the foundation for manipulating and analyzing your data.

Chapter 2: Understanding Data Types and Structures in R

Overview

In this chapter, we will dive into the foundational building blocks of data manipulation in R. Understanding the basic data types and structures is essential for working efficiently with data in R. We'll cover the most important data types like numeric, character, logical, and factors. Then, we'll explore the different data structures available in R—vectors, matrices, arrays, data frames, and lists—and learn when to use each one. Finally, we will work through a real-world example of creating and manipulating a data frame to analyze customer data.

Data Types in R

R, like other programming languages, has different types of data, and knowing how to work with these types is essential for data manipulation and analysis. Below are the primary data types in R:

Numeric

Numeric data types represent numbers. In R, all numbers by default are treated as **numeric** (which includes both integers and real numbers). For example:

r

```
x <- 42      # Numeric (integer)

y <- 3.14    # Numeric (real number)
```

You can perform mathematical operations such as addition, subtraction, multiplication, and division with numeric data types.

r

```
sum <- x + y

product <- x * y
```

Character

Character data types are used to store text or string data. Any data enclosed in quotation marks (either single ' or double ") is considered a character string.

r

```
name <- "John"

city <- 'New York'
```

Character variables can be used to represent names, categories, addresses, and other textual data.

Logical

The logical data type in R represents boolean values—either TRUE or FALSE. It is often used in conditional statements and comparisons.

r

is_adult <- TRUE

has_children <- FALSE

Logical values are important in data analysis for filtering and making decisions based on conditions.

Factors

Factors are used to represent categorical data. They are similar to character data types but with added functionality. A factor is an R object that represents categorical data with a fixed set of unique values called levels. Factors are particularly useful in statistical modeling.

r

gender <- factor(c("Male", "Female", "Female", "Male"))

Factors allow R to treat categorical data efficiently, especially when performing analyses like regression or plotting, where R can recognize the levels of the factor.

Factors can be ordered or unordered. An **ordered factor** might represent data like "Low," "Medium," and "High," while an **unordered factor** represents categories like "Male" and "Female."

r

```
education <- factor(c("Bachelor", "Master",
"Doctorate"), ordered = TRUE)
```

Data Structures in R

In R, there are several data structures that help in organizing and managing data. These include vectors, matrices, arrays, data frames, and lists. Each of these data structures has its own specific purpose and is suited for different types of data.

Vectors

A **vector** is the simplest data structure in R, consisting of a sequence of elements of the same data type. Vectors can be created using the c() function (short for **combine**). For example:

r

```
numbers <- c(1, 2, 3, 4, 5)
```

Vectors can be of any data type:

r

```r
char_vector <- c("apple", "banana", "cherry")

bool_vector <- c(TRUE, FALSE, TRUE)
```

You can access elements in a vector by indexing:

r

```r
first_element <- numbers[1]   # Accesses the first element
```

Vectors are a powerful tool for storing and manipulating ordered data. Most R functions expect data in the form of a vector.

Matrices

A **matrix** is a two-dimensional data structure that holds elements of the same type. It is similar to a vector but with rows and columns. You can create a matrix using the matrix() function:

r

```r
m <- matrix(1:6, nrow = 2, ncol = 3)
```

This creates a matrix with 2 rows and 3 columns, populated by the numbers from 1 to 6.

You can access individual elements using row and column indices:

r

```r
element <- m[1, 2]   # Accesses the element at the
```
first row, second column

Matrices are especially useful when dealing with mathematical operations, such as linear algebra.

Arrays

An **array** is similar to a matrix but can have more than two dimensions (n-dimensional). Arrays are created using the array() function. For example, a 3-dimensional array can be created as follows:

r

```r
arr <- array(1:12, dim = c(2, 3, 2))  # 2 rows, 3
```
columns, 2 layers

You can access elements in an array by specifying the indices for each dimension:

r

```r
element <- arr[1, 2, 1]   # First row, second column,
```
first layer

Arrays are ideal for representing multidimensional data, such as 3D data sets or image data.

Data Frames

A **data frame** is one of the most important data structures in R and is used for storing data in a table format. Each column in a data frame can hold a different data type (e.g., numeric, character, factor), making data frames highly versatile for storing mixed data types.

You can create a data frame using the data.frame() function:

r

```
df <- data.frame(
  Name = c("John", "Jane", "Alice"),
  Age = c(30, 25, 35),
  City = c("New York", "Los Angeles", "Chicago")
)
```

Data frames are extremely useful in data science and machine learning workflows because they allow for efficient storage and manipulation of data. You can access individual columns using the $ operator or by indexing:

r

```
df$Name      # Accesses the 'Name' column
df[1, 2]     # Accesses the first row, second column
```

Data frames also allow for powerful data manipulation techniques with packages like dplyr and tidyr, which enable operations such as filtering, grouping, and summarizing.

Lists

A **list** in R is a versatile data structure that can hold different types of elements, including other lists, vectors, matrices, and even functions. Lists are created using the list() function:

r

```
my_list <- list(
  Name = "John",
  Age = 30,
  Scores = c(95, 88, 76),
  Address = list(City = "New York", Zip = 10001)
)
```

Unlike vectors, lists allow elements of different types. You can access individual elements of a list using the [[ ]] or $ operator:

r

```
my_list[[1]]      # Accesses the first element
my_list$Age       # Accesses the 'Age' element
```

Lists are often used in R for complex data structures, such as modeling or nested data sets.

Real-World Example: Creating and Manipulating Data Frames for Customer Data Analysis

Let's now walk through a real-world example to demonstrate how to create and manipulate data frames in R for a customer data analysis scenario.

Step 1: Create a Sample Customer Data Frame

Imagine you work for a retail company and want to analyze customer data. The data frame might contain customer information such as name, age, gender, and total spend. Let's create this data frame:

r

```r
customer_data <- data.frame(
  CustomerID = c(101, 102, 103, 104, 105),
  Name = c("Alice", "Bob", "Charlie", "David", "Eva"),
  Age = c(25, 30, 35, 40, 28),
  Gender = factor(c("Female", "Male", "Male", "Male", "Female")),
  TotalSpend = c(500, 1500, 2000, 800, 1200)
)

print(customer_data)
```

This will produce the following output:

yaml

	CustomerID	Name	Age	Gender	TotalSpend
1	101	Alice	25	Female	500
2	102	Bob	30	Male	1500
3	103	Charlie	35	Male	2000
4	104	David	40	Male	800
5	105	Eva	28	Female	1200

Step 2: Summarize the Data

Now, let's calculate some basic statistics to understand the data better, such as the average age of customers and the total spending:

r

```r
mean_age <- mean(customer_data$Age)
total_spending <- sum(customer_data$TotalSpend)

cat("The average age of customers is:", mean_age, "\n")
cat("The total spending across all customers is:", total_spending)
```

Step 3: Filter and Subset Data

You may want to analyze specific groups of customers. For example, you might want to extract data for customers who have spent over $1000. You can do this using the subset() function or using dplyr:

r

```r
high_spending_customers <- subset(customer_data, TotalSpend > 1000)

print(high_spending_customers)
```

This will display:

yaml

```yaml
  CustomerID   Name Age Gender TotalSpend
2     102    Bob 30   Male      1500
3     103 Charlie 35   Male      2000
5     105    Eva 28 Female      1200
```

Step 4: Add a New Column

You may want to add a new column to your data frame. For instance, you could add a column to indicate whether each customer is a "high spender" or not, based on their total spending:

r

```r
customer_data$HighSpender <- ifelse(customer_data$TotalSpend > 1000, "Yes", "No")
```

```
print(customer_data)
```

This will append the new column to the data frame:

yaml

	CustomerID	Name	Age	Gender	TotalSpend	HighSpender
1	101	Alice	25	Female	500	No
2	102	Bob	30	Male	1500	Yes
3	103	Charlie	35	Male	2000	Yes
4	104	David	40	Male	800	No
5	105	Eva	28	Female	1200	Yes

In this chapter, we covered the fundamental data types and structures in R, which form the backbone of data manipulation and analysis. Understanding how to work with vectors, matrices, arrays, data frames, and lists is essential for any data scientist or machine learning practitioner. We also explored the creation and manipulation of data frames using a real-world example involving customer data analysis.

By now, you should be comfortable with how to create and manipulate different types of data structures in R, as well as how to begin performing basic data analysis operations. In the next chapter, we'll explore data cleaning and transformation, which are essential skills for preparing data for machine learning models.

Chapter 3: Data Cleaning and Preprocessing

Overview

In any data analysis or machine learning workflow, **data cleaning and preprocessing** are crucial steps. Raw data often comes with missing values, outliers, inconsistencies, and other imperfections that can hinder accurate analysis or model training. To ensure that data is in a usable form, it's important to clean and preprocess it before applying any statistical techniques or algorithms. This chapter will guide you through the key steps in data cleaning and preprocessing, including handling missing values, dealing with outliers, and performing data transformations like scaling and normalization. We'll conclude by walking through a real-world example of cleaning sales data.

Handling Missing Values

In real-world datasets, it's common to encounter **missing values** (NaNs or NAs), which may occur due to incomplete data collection, system errors, or various other reasons. Missing data can lead to biased results or errors in your analysis or models if not handled properly. There are several strategies to handle missing values in R, depending on the nature of the data and the analysis goals.

Identifying Missing Values

In R, missing values are represented by NA. You can check for missing values using the is.na() function. For example:

r

```
# Example data
sales_data <- data.frame(
  ProductID = c(1, 2, 3, 4, 5),
  Sales = c(500, NA, 700, 800, NA),
  Region = c("North", "South", "East", "West", "North")
)
```

```
# Check for missing values
is.na(sales_data$Sales)
```

This will return a logical vector (TRUE for missing values, FALSE for non-missing values):

graphql

```
[1] FALSE  TRUE FALSE FALSE  TRUE
```

Handling Missing Data

Once missing values are identified, you can choose how to handle them. Common approaches include:

1. Removing Missing Values

If the amount of missing data is small, you might consider removing rows or columns containing missing values. Use the na.omit() function or drop_na() from the tidyr package:

r

```
# Remove rows with missing data
cleaned_data <- na.omit(sales_data)
```

Alternatively, to remove columns with missing values:

r

```
cleaned_data <- sales_data[,
colSums(is.na(sales_data)) == 0]
```

2. Imputing Missing Values

In many cases, removing missing data may lead to the loss of valuable information, especially if missing values are widespread. An alternative is **imputation**, which involves filling in the missing values using some statistical method.

For numerical data, common imputation strategies include replacing missing values with:

- The **mean** or **median** of the column
- The **mode** (most frequent value) for categorical data

Example using the dplyr package for replacing missing values with the mean:

r

```
library(dplyr)

sales_data <- sales_data %>%
  mutate(Sales = ifelse(is.na(Sales), mean(Sales, na.rm = TRUE), Sales))
```

Alternatively, for imputing categorical data, you can replace missing values with the **mode**:

r

```
mode_impute <- function(x) {
  # Find the most frequent value (mode)
  mode_value <- as.character(names(sort(table(x), decreasing = TRUE))[1])
  return(mode_value)
}
```

```
sales_data$Region[is.na(sales_data$Region)] <-
mode_impute(sales_data$Region)
```

3. Advanced Imputation Techniques

For more advanced imputation, techniques such as **K-nearest neighbors (KNN)** imputation, or using machine learning models, may be employed, especially for larger datasets or when relationships between variables are important. The impute package or caret package can be used for such purposes.

Handling Outliers

Outliers are data points that deviate significantly from other observations in the dataset. These extreme values can distort statistical analyses and machine learning models, leading to inaccurate results. Detecting and handling outliers is an important part of the preprocessing pipeline.

Identifying Outliers

There are several methods to identify outliers in R. One common approach is using statistical techniques like the **Interquartile Range (IQR)** or **Z-scores**.

1. Interquartile Range (IQR)

The IQR method identifies outliers based on the range between the 1st and 3rd quartiles (Q1 and Q3). Outliers are typically defined as values below

$Q1 - 1.5 \times IQR$ or above $Q3 + 1.5 \times IQR$.

r

```
# Calculate IQR

IQR_value <- IQR(sales_data$Sales, na.rm = TRUE)

Q1 <- quantile(sales_data$Sales, 0.25, na.rm = TRUE)

Q3 <- quantile(sales_data$Sales, 0.75, na.rm = TRUE)


# Determine outlier thresholds

lower_bound <- Q1 - 1.5 * IQR_value

upper_bound <- Q3 + 1.5 * IQR_value


# Identify outliers

outliers <- sales_data$Sales[sales_data$Sales < lower_bound | sales_data$Sales > upper_bound]

outliers
```

2. Z-Score Method

Z-scores measure how many standard deviations a data point is from the mean. Values with a Z-score greater than 3 (or less than -3) are typically considered outliers.

r

```r
z_scores <- scale(sales_data$Sales)
outliers <- sales_data$Sales[abs(z_scores) > 3]
outliers
```

Handling Outliers

Once outliers are identified, you have several options for handling them:

- **Remove**: If the outliers are due to errors, you might consider removing them.

- **Cap**: For valid outliers, you can use **capping**, where values beyond a certain threshold are replaced with the threshold value.

- **Transformation**: Sometimes transforming the data (e.g., using a logarithmic or square root transformation) can reduce the impact of outliers.

Example of capping outliers:

r

```r
sales_data$Sales[sales_data$Sales > upper_bound] <- upper_bound
```

```r
sales_data$Sales[sales_data$Sales < lower_bound]
<- lower_bound
```

Data Transformation Techniques

Data transformation is often necessary to ensure that the data is in the right format and scale for analysis. Two common transformations in machine learning are **scaling** and **normalization**.

Scaling

Scaling involves adjusting the range of your data to ensure that variables are on a similar scale, which is important for distance-based algorithms like KNN or gradient-based algorithms like linear regression or neural networks.

In R, you can scale data using the scale() function, which centers the data around the mean (zero) and scales it by the standard deviation (unit variance).

```r
r
```

```r
scaled_sales <- scale(sales_data$Sales)
```

Normalization

Normalization involves rescaling the data to a specific range, usually between 0 and 1. This can be helpful for algorithms that rely on the assumption that all features are on a similar scale, such as neural networks.

You can normalize data manually by subtracting the minimum value and dividing by the range:

r

```
normalized_sales <- (sales_data$Sales - min(sales_data$Sales)) / (max(sales_data$Sales) - min(sales_data$Sales))
```

Alternatively, the caret package provides a function for normalization:

r

```
library(caret)

normalized_data <- preProcess(sales_data, method = "range")

sales_data_normalized <- predict(normalized_data, sales_data)
```

Real-World Example: Cleaning Sales Data for Analysis

Let's apply the concepts we've discussed by cleaning a sales dataset. Suppose you work for a retail company and are tasked with analyzing monthly sales data. The data contains some missing values, outliers, and different scales across variables. Below is a step-by-step guide for cleaning and preprocessing this data.

Step 1: Load the Data

r

```
sales_data <- data.frame(

  Month = c("January", "February", "March", "April", "May"),

  Sales = c(500, NA, 1200, 15000, 800),

  Region = c("North", "South", "North", "West", "East"),

  Discount = c(5, 10, 15, 50, 5)

)
```

Step 2: Handle Missing Values

For simplicity, let's impute the missing sales value with the mean sales value:

r

```
sales_data$Sales[is.na(sales_data$Sales)] <- mean(sales_data$Sales, na.rm = TRUE)
```

Step 3: Detect and Handle Outliers

Using the IQR method, we'll detect and cap extreme values in the sales data:

r

```r
IQR_value <- IQR(sales_data$Sales)

Q1 <- quantile(sales_data$Sales, 0.25)

Q3 <- quantile(sales_data$Sales, 0.75)

lower_bound <- Q1 - 1.5 * IQR_value

upper_bound <- Q3 + 1.5 * IQR_value


# Cap outliers

sales_data$Sales[sales_data$Sales > upper_bound]
<- upper_bound

sales_data$Sales[sales_data$Sales < lower_bound]
<- lower_bound
```

Step 4: Normalize the Sales Data

Finally, let's normalize the sales values to a 0-1 range:

r

```r
sales_data$NormalizedSales <- (sales_data$Sales -
min(sales_data$Sales)) / (max(sales_data$Sales) -
min(sales_data$Sales))
```

Data cleaning and preprocessing are essential steps to ensure your data is suitable for analysis or modeling. In this chapter, we explored strategies for handling missing values, detecting and dealing with outliers, and transforming data using scaling and normalization. By following these steps, you can prepare your dataset for more accurate and reliable analysis.

Chapter 4: Data Manipulation with dplyr and tidyr

Overview

Data manipulation is a core aspect of working with data. R provides powerful packages for data manipulation, and two of the most popular ones are dplyr and tidyr. These packages, both part of the **tidyverse**, offer a rich set of tools for transforming and reshaping data. They are widely used by data scientists and analysts for tasks such as filtering, grouping, summarizing, and reshaping data to meet the needs of analysis or machine learning.

In this chapter, we will introduce you to both dplyr and tidyr, focusing on their core functions for manipulating and transforming data. We will also explore real-world examples to help you understand how to apply these packages to clean, reshape, and analyze data. Specifically, we'll use employee performance data as our example to demonstrate how to use dplyr and tidyr for common data manipulation tasks.

Introduction to dplyr and tidyr Packages

Before diving into data manipulation tasks, let's first understand the basics of the dplyr and tidyr packages.

1. dplyr: A Grammar of Data Manipulation

dplyr is a powerful package designed to provide a simple and consistent interface for data manipulation tasks. It is centered around a set of intuitive verbs that help you perform common tasks such as selecting, filtering, and summarizing data. Here are some of the most common functions in dplyr:

- **filter()**: Select rows based on condition(s).
- **select()**: Choose columns based on their names.
- **mutate()**: Add or modify columns.
- **arrange()**: Sort the data based on one or more columns.
- **summarize() (or summarise())**: Condense data into summary statistics.
- **group_by()**: Group data for summarization or aggregation.

2. tidyr: Tidying Up Your Data

While dplyr helps with row and column manipulation, tidyr focuses on reshaping and tidying your data. It helps in transforming data from a messy format into a tidy format, which is essential for analysis in R. Tidy data has a consistent structure where each variable is a column, each observation is a row, and each type of observational unit is a table.

Common functions in tidyr include:

- **gather()**: Convert wide data to long format.

- **spread()**: Convert long data to wide format.

- **separate()**: Split a single column into multiple columns.

- **unite()**: Combine multiple columns into one.

Together, dplyr and tidyr offer a comprehensive toolkit for manipulating and reshaping your data, making it more suitable for analysis.

Filtering, Grouping, and Summarizing Data with dplyr and tidyr

1. Filtering Data with filter()

Filtering data allows you to subset your data based on certain conditions. The filter() function in dplyr is used to select rows that meet specific criteria. Here's an example of how you might filter employee performance data to focus on employees who have exceeded a certain performance threshold.

r

```r
library(dplyr)

# Sample employee performance data
employee_data <- data.frame(
  EmployeeID = c(101, 102, 103, 104, 105),
  Name = c("Alice", "Bob", "Charlie", "David", "Eva"),
  PerformanceScore = c(85, 92, 78, 95, 88),
  Department = c("Sales", "Marketing", "Sales", "HR", "Sales")
)

# Filter employees with performance scores greater than 85
high_performers <- filter(employee_data, PerformanceScore > 85)
print(high_performers)
```

This returns:

	EmployeeID	Name	PerformanceScore	Department
1	102	Bob	92	Marketing
2	104	David	95	HR
3	105	Eva	88	Sales

You can also filter based on multiple conditions. For example, selecting high-performing employees from the Sales department:

r

```
high_performers_sales <- filter(employee_data,
PerformanceScore > 85 & Department == "Sales")

print(high_performers_sales)
```

---

2. Grouping and Summarizing Data with group_by() and summarize()

In many cases, you need to aggregate or summarize your data based on different categories or groups. The combination of group_by() and summarize() allows you to group the data by one or more columns and then compute summary statistics for each group.

For example, let's calculate the average performance score for each department:

r

```
# Group by department and summarize average performance score

summary_data <- employee_data %>%

  group_by(Department) %>%

  summarize(AverageScore =
mean(PerformanceScore))
```

```
print(summary_data)
```

This returns:

perl

```
# A tibble: 3 × 2
  Department AverageScore
  <chr>           <dbl>
1 HR                 95
2 Marketing          92
3 Sales            84.3
```

Here, the data is grouped by the Department column, and the average performance score is calculated for each department.

You can also use other summary statistics, such as sum, median, standard deviation, and more:

r

```
# Summarize total performance score by department
total_score <- employee_data %>%
  group_by(Department) %>%
  summarize(TotalScore = sum(PerformanccScore))
print(total_score)
```

This would provide the total performance score for each department.

---

3. Creating and Modifying Columns with mutate()

The mutate() function allows you to create new columns or modify existing ones based on operations performed on the data. For example, let's add a new column that classifies employees based on their performance score.

r

```
# Add a new column 'PerformanceLevel' based on PerformanceScore

employee_data <- employee_data %>%

  mutate(PerformanceLevel = ifelse(PerformanceScore > 90, "Excellent",

                  ifelse(PerformanceScore > 80, "Good", "Needs Improvement")))

print(employee_data)
```

This would result in:

mathematica

EmployeeID	Name	PerformanceScore	Department	PerformanceLevel
1	101 Alice	85	Sales	Good

2	102	Bob	92	Marketing	Excellent
3	103	Charlie	78	Sales	Needs Improvement
4	104	David	95	HR	Excellent
5	105	Eva	88	Sales	Good

In this case, a new column PerformanceLevel is added based on the performance scores.

---

4. Reshaping Data with tidyr

4.1 Converting Data from Wide to Long Format with gather()

Sometimes, your data might be in a wide format (where each variable is a column), and you need to reshape it into a long format (where each row represents a single observation for a particular variable). gather() is used for this transformation.

Suppose you have monthly performance data for employees:

r


```
# Sample wide-format data

monthly_performance <- data.frame(

  EmployeeID = c(101, 102, 103, 104, 105),

  Jan = c(85, 92, 78, 95, 88),

  Feb = c(87, 94, 80, 97, 90),
```

```
  Mar = c(90, 95, 82, 99, 92)

)
```

Gather data from wide to long format

```
long_data <- gather(monthly_performance, key = "Month", value = "PerformanceScore", Jan:Mar)

print(long_data)
```

This will reshape the data so that you have one column for Month and another for PerformanceScore:

python

	EmployeeID	Month	PerformanceScore
1	101	Jan	85
2	102	Jan	92
3	103	Jan	78
4	104	Jan	95
5	105	Jan	88
6	101	Feb	87
7	102	Feb	94

...

Now, each employee's performance is captured in a long format, where each row corresponds to a specific month.

4.2 Converting Data from Long to Wide Format with spread()

If you need to go the other way, from long to wide format, you can use spread(). Here's how you could transform the previous long dataset back into a wide format:

r

```
# Spread data back to wide format

wide_data <- spread(long data, key = "Month", value = "PerformanceScore")

print(wide_data)
```

This will return the original wide-format data.

---

5. Handling Missing Values with tidyr

Another useful feature of tidyr is its ability to handle missing values. For example, the fill() function can be used to fill missing values in a dataset with the previous non-missing value.

r

```
# Fill missing performance scores with the previous available score

long_data_with_missing <- data.frame(

  EmployeeID = c(101, 102, 103, 104, 105),
```

```
  Month = c("Jan", "Jan", "Feb", "Feb", "Mar"),

  PerformanceScore = c(85, NA, 78, NA, 90)

)


long_data_filled <- long_data_with_missing %>%

  fill(PerformanceScore, .direction = "down")

print(long_data_filled)
```

This would fill the missing PerformanceScore values with the previous available score.

In this chapter, we explored how to manipulate and reshape data using dplyr and tidyr—two of the most powerful packages in R for data manipulation. We covered core functions for filtering, grouping, summarizing, creating new columns, and reshaping data. By using these functions, you can transform your raw data into a form that is more useful for analysis and machine learning.

Chapter 5:
Exploratory Data
Analysis (EDA)

Overview

Exploratory Data Analysis (EDA) is one of the most crucial steps in the data science process. It involves analyzing a dataset to summarize its main characteristics, often with visual methods. EDA is the foundation of data analysis, allowing you to better understand your dataset, detect patterns, uncover relationships, identify anomalies, and check assumptions. The insights gleaned from EDA can guide you in formulating hypotheses, cleaning data, and even selecting machine learning algorithms.

This chapter will provide an in-depth overview of EDA techniques, focusing on data visualization and summarization techniques that help in understanding data distributions, relationships, and statistical properties. We will apply these methods to a real-world example, analyzing a dataset of online retail sales to uncover trends, patterns, and insights.

Introduction to Exploratory Data Analysis (EDA)

What is EDA?

Exploratory Data Analysis (EDA) refers to the initial steps of data analysis where you use a variety of statistical and graphical methods to explore and understand the structure of your data. EDA helps you to:

- **Identify patterns**: Discover trends and relationships within the data.

- **Understand distributions**: Visualize how individual variables are distributed.

- **Spot anomalies**: Identify outliers or missing data.

- **Check assumptions**: Test the validity of assumptions that underlie the modeling process.

While EDA is not about proving a hypothesis, it is about generating hypotheses and building an intuition for the data. Visualizations are a key tool in this process.

Importance of EDA

In data science, EDA serves several critical purposes:

1. **Data Cleaning**: Helps detect missing values, duplicates, and inconsistencies.

2. **Hypothesis Generation**: Uncovers trends and relationships that can form the basis for future analysis or hypothesis testing.

3. **Data Transformation**: Guides decisions on how to preprocess data for machine learning models (e.g., normalization, encoding).

4. **Modeling Assumptions**: Helps determine the statistical assumptions underlying machine learning algorithms and suggests adjustments.

By understanding these aspects, you can perform more effective data analysis and build more accurate models.

Data Visualization: An Overview

Data visualization is one of the most powerful tools in EDA. Through visual representations of data, patterns that are not immediately obvious in raw data can become clear. The **ggplot2** package in R is an excellent tool for creating a variety of plots to visualize data distributions and relationships.

Common Visualization Techniques

1. **Histograms**: Useful for understanding the distribution of a single numerical variable. A histogram shows how data points are distributed across a continuous range.

2. **Boxplots**: Excellent for showing the distribution of data, especially with regard to

outliers and the spread (interquartile range) of data.

3. **Scatter Plots**: Best for visualizing relationships between two continuous variables, useful for spotting correlations.

4. **Bar Plots**: Ideal for displaying categorical data and comparing frequencies across categories.

5. **Correlation Heatmaps**: A matrix of scatter plots or color-coded cells that shows the strength of relationships between multiple variables.

6. **Pair Plots**: A matrix of scatter plots to show the relationships between several variables in a dataset.

Key Steps in Data Visualization for EDA

- **Exploring the Distribution**: How the data is spread out (mean, median, range, etc.).

- **Exploring Relationships**: How different variables relate to each other.

- **Identifying Outliers**: Detecting unusual or extreme values in the data.

- **Visualizing Missing Data**: Identifying missing or incomplete values in your dataset.

Summarizing and Exploring Statistical Properties of Datasets

Before jumping into complex models, it's important to understand the basic statistical properties of the dataset. This includes:

1. Summary Statistics

Summary statistics provide a concise description of the data. In R, the summary() function provides essential information such as the minimum, maximum, median, mean, and quartiles of numerical variables.

r

Summary statistics for the dataset

summary(retail_data)

This will return the following types of statistics:

- **Min, Max**: The range of values for each variable.

- **Median, Mean**: Central tendency measures.

- **1st Quartile (Q1), 3rd Quartile (Q3)**: Represent the spread of the data.

2. Central Tendency

- **Mean**: The average value of a variable. While simple, the mean can be influenced by outliers.

r

Mean of sales in retail data

mean(retail_data$Sales, na.rm = TRUE)

- **Median**: The middle value when the data is sorted. Unlike the mean, the median is less sensitive to outliers.

r

Median of sales

median(retail_data$Sales, na.rm = TRUE)

- **Mode**: The most frequent value in a dataset. The mode can be useful when dealing with categorical data.

3. Variance and Standard Deviation

Variance measures the spread of data points around the mean. Standard deviation is the square root of variance and gives a more interpretable measure of spread.

r

Standard deviation of sales

sd(retail_data$Sales, na.rm = TRUE)

Variance and standard deviation can help you understand the consistency of sales figures, for example.

Real-World Example: EDA on a Dataset of Online Retail Sales

Now, let's put these concepts into practice with a real-world example. Imagine you have a dataset that contains sales data from an online retail store. The dataset includes several columns, such as:

- **OrderID**: Unique identifier for each order.

- **ProductID**: Identifier for the product sold.

- **Quantity**: The number of units sold in each order.

- **Price**: The price of the product.

- **Sales**: Total sales value (Quantity × Price).

- **OrderDate**: Date when the order was placed.

Let's walk through the steps of performing EDA on this dataset using R.

Step 1: Load and Explore the Dataset

r

```r
# Load necessary libraries
library(ggplot2)
library(dplyr)
library(tidyr)
```

```r
# Load the online retail sales dataset

retail_data <- read.csv("retail_sales.csv")


# View the first few rows of the dataset

head(retail_data)
```

This will give us a glimpse into the structure of the dataset.

Step 2: Visualize the Distribution of Sales

Histogram of Sales

To get an idea of how sales are distributed across orders, we can create a histogram of the Sales column:

r

```r
# Plot histogram of sales

ggplot(retail_data, aes(x = Sales)) +

  geom_histogram(binwidth = 5, fill = "lightblue", color = "black") +

  labs(title = "Sales Distribution", x = "Sales", y = "Frequency")
```

This histogram shows how the sales are distributed. From this, we can identify if there are any skewed distributions or outliers in the sales data.

Boxplot of Sales

A boxplot is another effective tool for visualizing the spread and identifying outliers.

r

```
# Boxplot of sales

ggplot(retail_data, aes(y = Sales)) +

  geom_boxplot(fill = "lightblue") +

  labs(title = "Sales Distribution (Boxplot)", y = "Sales")
```

This boxplot will display the median, quartiles, and any potential outliers in the sales data.

Step 3: Investigate Relationships Between Variables

Scatter Plot of Quantity vs. Sales

Next, we want to explore the relationship between Quantity and Sales to understand how they are related. A scatter plot is perfect for this.

r

```
# Scatter plot of Quantity vs Sales

ggplot(retail_data, aes(x = Quantity, y = Sales)) +

  geom_point(color = "blue") +

  labs(title = "Quantity vs. Sales", x = "Quantity", y = "Sales")
```

This scatter plot allows us to see whether there is a linear relationship between the quantity of items sold and the total sales value.

Correlation Matrix

To examine the relationships between multiple numeric variables, a correlation matrix can be helpful. We will look at the correlation between Quantity, Price, and Sales.

r

```
# Correlation matrix

correlation_matrix <- cor(retail_data[, c("Quantity", "Price", "Sales")], use = "complete.obs")

print(correlation_matrix)
```

This will return the correlation values, helping us understand how these variables relate to one another. A positive correlation between Quantity and Sales suggests that higher quantities generally result in higher sales.

Step 4: Missing Data Analysis

Before proceeding to modeling or further analysis, it's important to check for missing values in the dataset.

r

```
# Check for missing data
```

sum(is.na(retail_data))

If there are missing values, you can decide whether to remove rows with missing data, impute missing values, or use another method depending on the extent of the missing data.

Step 5: Grouped Summary Statistics

Finally, you can use grouping functions to summarize the data based on categories, such as sales by product.

r


```
# Group by ProductID and summarize sales

sales_by_product <- retail_data %>%

  group_by(ProductID) %>%

  summarize(TotalSales = sum(Sales, na.rm = TRUE),

      AverageSales = mean(Sales, na.rm = TRUE))

print(sales_by_product)
```

This summary will give us the total and average sales for each product in the store.

Exploratory Data Analysis is an essential process for any data scientist or analyst. It allows you to understand the data, uncover patterns, relationships, and anomalies, and prepare the data for further analysis or modeling. Through visualizations like histograms, boxplots, and scatter plots, along with summary statistics, EDA helps provide a clear overview of the dataset.

In the real-world example of analyzing retail sales data, EDA allowed us to uncover trends, visualize distributions, and investigate relationships between variables. These insights will guide the next steps in the analysis, whether it's cleaning the data, transforming variables, or selecting machine learning algorithms.

Chapter 6: Data Visualization with ggplot2

Overview

Data visualization is a key aspect of data analysis, as it allows you to communicate your findings and insights effectively. Visualizing complex data through graphs and plots makes it easier to identify patterns, relationships, trends, and outliers that might not be immediately apparent from raw data. In this chapter, we will explore **ggplot2**, one of the most popular R packages for data visualization, to create static and dynamic plots. Additionally, we will focus on customizing plots to improve clarity, aesthetics, and overall presentation.

We will also work through a real-world example of **visualizing stock price trends over time**. This example will demonstrate how to apply ggplot2 to financial data and create visualizations that can help investors and analysts interpret market movements.

Introduction to ggplot2

What is ggplot2?

ggplot2 is a powerful and flexible R package for creating visualizations based on the principles of **Grammar of Graphics**, which was introduced by Hadley Wickham. It provides a consistent way to describe and create visualizations by breaking down the process into manageable components:

1. **Data**: The dataset being visualized.

2. **Aesthetics**: How the data is represented visually (e.g., axes, colors, shapes).

3. **Geometries**: The type of plot (e.g., points, lines, bars).

4. **Statistical transformations**: How the data should be summarized (e.g., smoothing, binning).

5. **Faceting**: Creating subplots based on the data's categorical variables.

6. **Coordinates**: The coordinate system for displaying the data (e.g., Cartesian, polar).

With ggplot2, you can create a wide variety of static and dynamic visualizations, ranging from basic bar charts to complex multi-plot arrangements. The intuitive syntax makes it easy to layer different components of a plot, and the package is highly customizable.

Advantages of ggplot2

- **Ease of use**: Once you understand the basic components, creating complex plots becomes straightforward.

- **Flexibility**: It supports a wide range of plot types and customization options.

- **Aesthetic quality**: ggplot2 produces publication-quality plots by default.

- **Integration with the tidyverse**: ggplot2 integrates seamlessly with other packages like dplyr and tidyr, which are commonly used in data preprocessing and manipulation.

Basic Syntax of ggplot2

The general syntax for creating plots with ggplot2 follows the structure:

r

```
ggplot(data, aes(x = variable1, y = variable2)) +
 geom_type()
```

Where:

- data is the dataset you're using for the plot.

- aes() defines the aesthetic mappings, like which variables to map to the x- and y-axes.

- geom_type() defines the type of plot, such as geom_point() for a scatter plot, geom_line() for a line plot, etc.

Install and Load ggplot2

Before using ggplot2, you need to install and load it. You can do this with the following commands:

r

```
# Install ggplot2 if you haven't already
install.packages("ggplot2")
```

```
# Load ggplot2
library(ggplot2)
```

Static Visualizations with ggplot2

1. Creating Basic Plots

Line Plot for Stock Price Trends

A line plot is an effective way to visualize the trend of a continuous variable over time. In our example, we'll visualize stock prices over time to observe trends, volatility, and patterns.

Here's how to create a simple line plot with ggplot2 to visualize stock price trends:

r

```
# Sample dataset: Stock price data
```

```r
stock_data <- data.frame(
  Date = seq(from = as.Date("2022-01-01"), by =
"month", length.out = 12),
  Price = c(100, 105, 110, 115, 120, 125, 130, 135,
140, 145, 150, 155)
)
```

```r
# Basic line plot of stock price over time
ggplot(stock_data, aes(x = Date, y = Price)) +
  geom_llne() +
  labs(title = "Stock Price Trends Over Time", x =
"Date", y = "Price") +
  theme_minimal()
```

This code creates a simple line plot that shows how the stock price changes over the year. The aes() function specifies that the x-axis will represent the Date and the y-axis will represent the Price. The geom_line() function adds a line connecting the data points.

Customizing Line Plot with Color and Style

We can enhance the line plot by customizing it with colors, line types, and other stylistic elements.

r

```r
# Line plot with customized color and line type
```

```r
ggplot(stock_data, aes(x = Date, y = Price)) +

  geom_line(color = "blue", linetype = "dashed", size =
1) +

  labs(title = "Stock Price Trends Over Time", x =
"Date", y = "Price") +

  theme_minimal()
```

This version uses a blue dashed line for the stock price and increases the line thickness to 1.

2. Bar Plot for Monthly Sales or Volume

Bar plots are useful for comparing quantities across different categories. For example, you might use a bar plot to compare the volume of stocks traded each month.

r

```r
# Sample dataset: Monthly trade volume

trade_data <- data.frame(

  Month = c("January", "February", "March", "April",
"May"),

  Volume = c(10000, 12000, 11000, 13000, 14000)

)


# Bar plot for monthly trade volume

ggplot(trade_data, aes(x = Month, y = Volume)) +
```

```r
geom_bar(stat = "identity", fill = "steelblue") +

labs(title = "Monthly Stock Trade Volume", x = "Month", y = "Volume") +

theme_minimal()
```

Here, the geom_bar() function creates a bar plot where the Volume is plotted against the Month.

Dynamic Visualizations with ggplot2

While ggplot2 is primarily designed for static visualizations, it can also be combined with other packages such as plotly or shiny to create dynamic and interactive visualizations.

1. Interactive Plots with Plotly

The plotly package enables interactive versions of ggplot2 plots, allowing users to hover, zoom, and click on elements for more detailed views. To install plotly, use the following:

r

```r
# Install plotly package
install.packages("plotly")
library(plotly)
```

```
# Create an interactive plot

ggplotly(

  ggplot(stock_data, aes(x = Date, y = Price)) +

    geom_line(color = "blue", size = 1) +

    labs(title = "Interactive Stock Price Trends Over
Time", x = "Date", y = "Price")

)
```

This converts the previously created ggplot2 line plot into an interactive plot, where users can zoom in on specific sections of the chart or hover to see the exact data points.

2. Adding Interactive Tooltips

You can add tooltips to ggplot2 plots using the plotly package to display additional information when hovering over data points.

r

```
# Create an interactive line plot with tooltips

ggplotly(

  ggplot(stock_data, aes(x = Date, y = Price, text =
paste("Price: $", Price))) +

    geom_line(color = "blue", size = 1) +

    labs(title = "Stock Price Trends with Tooltips", x =
"Date", y = "Price")

)
```

This code adds a tooltip that displays the stock price when the user hovers over any data point.

Customizing ggplot2 Plots

One of the most powerful features of ggplot2 is the ability to customize every aspect of your plot, from colors and labels to themes and legends.

1. Customizing Colors

You can customize the color of your plots using the fill and color arguments. For example, if you want to change the color of a line plot:

r

```
# Line plot with customized color
ggplot(stock_data, aes(x = Date, y = Price)) +
  geom_line(color = "green", size = 1) +
  labs(title = "Stock Price Trends (Green Line)", x = "Date", y = "Price") +
  theme_minimal()
```

2. Customizing Titles and Labels

You can add custom titles and labels to your plots to make them more descriptive.

r

```
# Custom titles and axis labels

ggplot(stock_data, aes(x = Date, y = Price)) +

  geom_line(color = "blue", size = 1) +

  labs(title = "Stock Price Trends for 2022", x = "Date",
y = "Price (USD)") +

  theme_minimal()
```

3. Modifying Themes

Themes in ggplot2 control the overall appearance of
the plot, including background color, gridlines, and
axis text. You can use predefined themes like
theme_minimal() or theme_light(), or customize them
further:

r

```
# Custom theme

ggplot(stock_data, aes(x = Date, y = Price)) +

  geom_line(color = "blue", size = 1) +

  labs(title = "Stock Price Trends with Custom
Theme", x = "Date", y = "Price") +

  theme_bw() +  # Black and white theme

  theme(

    axis.text.x = element_text(angle = 45, hjust = 1), #
Rotate x-axis labels
```

```
    plot.title = element_text(hjust = 0.5) # Center title
)
```

Real-World Example: Visualizing Stock Price Trends

To demonstrate the power of ggplot2 in a real-world scenario, let's walk through the process of visualizing stock price trends over time using a dataset that includes daily closing prices of a stock.

Step 1: Import Stock Data

You can either load stock price data from a CSV file, pull data from an API like Yahoo Finance, or use simulated data for the example.

r

```
# Importing stock data from a CSV file

stock_data <- read.csv("stock_data.csv")


# Convert Date column to Date type

stock_data$Date <- as.Date(stock_data$Date, format = "%Y-%m-%d")
```

Step 2: Create the Line Plot

Once the data is loaded, use ggplot2 to create a line plot of stock prices over time:

r

```
# Line plot of stock prices

ggplot(stock_data, aes(x = Date, y = ClosingPrice)) +

  geom_line(color = "blue") +

  labs(title = "Stock Price Trends (2022)", x = "Date", y = "Price (USD)") +

  theme_minimal()
```

Step 3: Analyze the Visualization

After visualizing the stock price trends, you can explore the plot to see if there are any significant fluctuations or patterns in the data. For instance, did the stock experience any sharp drops or increases at certain points in time? Is there any seasonal trend in the stock price?

Data visualization with **ggplot2** is an indispensable tool for any data scientist or analyst. It enables you to turn raw data into insightful, clear, and impactful visuals that can help inform decisions and tell compelling stories. In this chapter, we've explored the basics of ggplot2, created static and dynamic visualizations, and customized plots for clarity and aesthetics. By understanding how to work with ggplot2, you can better analyze stock price trends, customer behavior, sales patterns, and more.

Chapter 7: Introduction to Statistical Models in R

Overview of Statistical Models in R

Statistical models are essential tools in data analysis, providing a framework to understand the relationships between variables. In R, statistical modeling is made easier by the vast number of packages and built-in functions that allow you to fit various types of models. Whether you're working with simple linear regression, more complex machine learning models, or time series forecasting, R provides powerful tools for statistical modeling.

This chapter introduces the concept of statistical models in R, covering two foundational models—**linear regression** and **logistic regression**—and demonstrates how to apply them using real-world data. The focus will be on interpreting these models and using them for prediction. A real-world example will guide you through using linear regression to predict house prices, giving practical insight into how statistical models can be applied.

Understanding Statistical Models

Statistical models are mathematical constructs used to represent data and help explain relationships between different variables. They are built on assumptions about how data behaves, and these assumptions help us draw conclusions and make predictions.

Types of Statistical Models

Statistical models can be broadly classified into:

1. **Linear models**: Used when the relationship between the dependent variable and independent variables is assumed to be linear.

    o Example: Linear regression, Analysis of Variance (ANOVA).

2. **Non-linear models**: Used when relationships are more complex and can't be represented by a straight line.

    o Example: Non-linear regression, Generalized Additive Models (GAMs).

3. **Logistic models**: Used when the dependent variable is categorical (e.g., binary outcomes).

    o Example: Logistic regression, Poisson regression.

4. **Time Series Models**: Used when data points are collected sequentially in time.

    o Example: ARIMA, Exponential Smoothing State Space Models.

For this chapter, we will focus on **linear regression** and **logistic regression** as they are the most commonly used models in data science, particularly in predictive modeling.

Fitting a Linear Regression Model

What is Linear Regression?

Linear regression is one of the most commonly used statistical models, particularly for predicting continuous numerical outcomes based on one or more predictor variables. The basic idea is to model the relationship between a dependent variable (also called the **response variable**) and one or more independent variables (also called **predictors** or **features**) by fitting a linear equation to the observed data.

The general form of a simple linear regression equation is:

$y = \beta_0 + \beta_1 x_1 + \epsilon$

Where:

- y is the dependent variable.

- x_1 is the independent variable.

- β_0 is the intercept.

- β_1\beta_1β_1 is the slope, which represents how much $y$$y$$y$ changes for a unit change in $x_1$$x_1$$x_1$.

- ϵ\epsilon$\epsilon$ is the error term, capturing the variance in $y$$y$$y$ that is not explained by $x_1$$x_1$$x_1$.

Fitting a Simple Linear Regression in R

The lm() function in R is used to fit linear regression models. It stands for **linear model** and is capable of fitting both simple and multiple regression models.

Steps to Fit a Linear Regression Model

1. **Prepare the Data**: Clean and preprocess the data, ensuring the dependent and independent variables are correctly formatted.

2. **Fit the Model**: Use lm() to fit the model to the data.

3. **Evaluate the Model**: Review the summary output to understand the model's performance and significance.

Here's an example where we use linear regression to predict house prices based on square footage:

r

Sample dataset: House price data

house_data <- data.frame(

```
  Square_Feet = c(1500, 1800, 2400, 3000, 3500,
4000),

  Price = c(400000, 450000, 500000, 550000, 600000,
650000)

)
```

```
# Fit a simple linear regression model

model <- lm(Price ~ Square_Feet, data = house_data)
```

```
# Display the summary of the model

summary(model)
```

Output Interpretation:

The summary(model) function will display several key statistics, including:

- **Coefficients**: These values represent the intercept (β_0\beta_0β_0) and slope (β_1\beta_1β_1) of the linear regression equation.

- **R-squared**: This statistic tells us how well the model fits the data. It represents the proportion of variance in the dependent variable that is explained by the model.

- **p-value**: This tells us whether the predictors in the model are statistically significant.

From the output, you can interpret whether the relationship between square footage and price is statistically significant and how well the model explains the variation in prices.

Making Predictions

Once the model is fit, you can use it to make predictions. For example, if you want to predict the price of a house with 2500 square feet:

r

```
# Predict the price for a house with 2500 square feet

predict(model, newdata = data.frame(Square_Feet = 2500))
```

This will output the predicted price based on the linear regression model.

Fitting a Logistic Regression Model

What is Logistic Regression?

Logistic regression is used when the dependent variable is categorical, often with two categories (binary outcomes). Unlike linear regression, which predicts continuous values, logistic regression predicts the probability of a certain class or category based on the independent variables.

The logistic regression equation uses the **logistic function** (also known as the sigmoid function), which ensures that the output is constrained between 0 and 1, making it suitable for probability estimates:

$p(y=1)=1+e-(\beta 0+\beta 1x1)1$

Where:

- $p(y=1)p(y=1)p(y=1)$ is the probability of the event occurring (e.g., the probability that a customer buys a product).

- $\beta 0\backslash beta\_0\beta 0$ is the intercept.

- $\beta 1\backslash beta\_1\beta 1$ is the coefficient that represents the influence of $x1x\_1x1$ on the log-odds of the event occurring.

Fitting a Logistic Regression Model in R

The glm() function in R is used for fitting generalized linear models, including logistic regression. The key difference between lm() and glm() is that glm() allows you to specify the **family** of the model (e.g., binomial for logistic regression).

Steps to Fit a Logistic Regression Model

1. **Prepare the Data**: The dependent variable should be a binary factor (0 or 1).

2. **Fit the Model**: Use glm() with the family = binomial argument to fit a logistic regression model.

3. **Evaluate the Model**: Review the output to understand the coefficients and significance.

Here's an example using logistic regression to predict whether a customer will buy a product based on age and income:

r

```
# Sample dataset: Customer data

customer_data <- data.frame(
  Age = c(25, 30, 35, 40, 45, 50),
  Income = c(40000, 50000, 60000, 70000, 80000, 90000),
  Buy = c(0, 0, 1, 1, 1, 1)
)


# Fit a logistic regression model

logit_model <- glm(Buy ~ Age + Income, family = binomial, data = customer_data)


# Display the summary of the model

summary(logit_model)
```

Output Interpretation:

The logistic regression model summary includes:

- **Coefficients**: These represent the log-odds of the outcome (in this case, buying the product) for each unit change in the predictor variables.

- **p-value**: Tells you whether each predictor is statistically significant.

- **Deviance**: A measure of model fit; smaller values indicate a better fit.

Making Predictions

Once the model is fitted, you can predict the probability of a customer buying the product given their age and income:

r

```
# Predict the probability of buying for a customer aged 38 with an income of $75,000

predict(logit_model, newdata = data.frame(Age = 38, Income = 75000), type = "response")
```

The type = "response" argument returns the predicted probability, which will be a value between 0 and 1.

Real-World Example: Predicting House Prices with Linear Regression

Now, let's walk through a real-world example where we use linear regression to predict house prices based on square footage. This example will demonstrate how to apply the concepts of fitting a linear regression model, evaluating the model's performance, and making predictions.

Step 1: Prepare the Data

We will use a dataset of house prices and their corresponding square footage. Here's how we prepare the data in R:

r

```
# Sample dataset: House price data
house_data <- data.frame(
  Square_Feet = c(1500, 1800, 2400, 3000, 3500, 4000),
  Price = c(400000, 450000, 500000, 550000, 600000, 650000)
)
```

Step 2: Fit the Linear Regression Model

We fit a linear regression model to predict Price based on Square_Feet:

r

```
# Fit the linear regression model
model <- lm(Price ~ Square_Feet, data = house_data)

# Display the summary of the model
```

```
summary(model)
```

Step 3: Evaluate the Model

Review the summary output to understand the relationship between square footage and price. The coefficients section will tell you the intercept and slope of the model. The R-squared value will indicate how well the model explains the variation in house prices.

Step 4: Make Predictions

Finally, we use the model to predict the price of a house with 2500 square feet:

r

```
# Predict the price for a house with 2500 square feet

predicted_price <- predict(model, newdata = data.frame(Square_Feet = 2500))

print(predicted_price)
```

This will give you the predicted house price for a house of 2500 square feet.

In this chapter, we introduced statistical models in R, specifically **linear regression** and **logistic regression**. These models are foundational to data analysis and machine learning, helping us make predictions based on historical data.

We demonstrated how to fit linear and logistic regression models using R, interpret the results, and make predictions. Through a real-world example of predicting house prices, we highlighted the practical applications of these models in solving business and data science problems.

As you continue your journey in data science and machine learning, mastering statistical models like linear and logistic regression will provide you with the tools needed to analyze and predict real-world data effectively. In the next chapter, we will explore **model evaluation techniques**, which will allow us to assess the accuracy and performance of our models in greater detail.

Chapter 8: Building Classification Models

Introduction to Classification Algorithms

Classification is one of the core tasks in machine learning, where the goal is to predict a categorical label or class for a given input. It's particularly useful when dealing with datasets where the output variable is discrete and categorical in nature. Classification problems are commonly encountered in a wide range of real-world applications, such as email spam detection, medical diagnosis, fraud detection, and customer churn prediction.

In this chapter, we will explore two popular classification algorithms—**Decision Trees** and **k-Nearest Neighbors (k-NN)**. These algorithms will be used to build models that can classify data points based on their features. We will also discuss the process of model evaluation to ensure that our classification models generalize well to unseen data.

Key Concepts in Classification

Before diving into specific algorithms, let's first understand the core concepts in classification:

1. **Training Set**: A dataset with known labels used to train the model.

2. **Test Set**: A separate dataset used to evaluate the performance of the model.

3. **Accuracy**: The percentage of correct predictions made by the model compared to the total number of predictions.

4. **Precision, Recall, and F1-Score**: Metrics used for imbalanced classification problems, where accuracy alone may not give a complete picture of model performance.

5. **Confusion Matrix**: A table that describes the performance of a classification model by comparing the predicted labels with the true labels.

Decision Trees for Classification

What is a Decision Tree?

A **Decision Tree** is a tree-like structure where each internal node represents a decision based on a feature, each branch represents an outcome of that decision, and each leaf node represents a class label. The goal of a decision tree is to split the data in such a way that the resulting subgroups are as pure as possible, meaning that the data within each subgroup should predominantly belong to a single class.

How Decision Trees Work

Decision trees use a method called **recursive binary splitting** to divide the dataset into smaller subsets. At each node, the algorithm selects the feature that results in the most informative split (i.e., the one that best separates the data into different classes). The process of splitting continues until a stopping condition is met, such as a maximum depth or a minimum number of samples per leaf.

The key idea behind decision trees is the **Gini impurity** or **information gain** (for classification tasks) that measures how well a feature splits the data. A lower Gini impurity means the data at a particular node is purer.

Fitting a Decision Tree in R

R provides the rpart package to fit decision tree models. The function rpart() is used to build a decision tree for classification. Let's walk through an example of using a decision tree to predict customer churn.

Step 1: Prepare the Data

We'll use a dataset containing customer information, where the target variable is whether the customer has churned (1) or not (0).

r

```
# Load required libraries

library(rpart)

library(rpart.plot)


# Sample dataset for customer churn
```

```r
customer_data <- data.frame(
  Age = c(25, 30, 35, 40, 45, 50),
  Income = c(40000, 50000, 60000, 70000, 80000, 90000),
  Churn = c(0, 0, 1, 0, 1, 1)
)


# Fit a decision tree model
churn_tree <- rpart(Churn ~ Age + Income, data = customer_data, method = "class")


# Visualize the decision tree
rpart.plot(churn_tree)
```

Step 2: Model Evaluation

The rpart function builds a classification tree, and the rpart.plot() function visualizes it. The tree shows how the decision splits at each node, based on the features (in this case, Age and Income), and how these splits lead to the final classification.

To evaluate the model, we can use a confusion matrix to compare the model's predictions with the actual values:

```r
r
```

```r
# Predict on the training data
```

```
predictions <- predict(churn_tree, type = "class")
```

Confusion matrix

```
table(Predicted = predictions, Actual =
customer_data$Churn)
```

The confusion matrix helps us understand how well the decision tree performed. It shows the number of true positives, false positives, true negatives, and false negatives, which can be used to calculate performance metrics like accuracy, precision, and recall.

---

k-Nearest Neighbors (k-NN) for Classification

What is k-NN?

k-Nearest Neighbors (k-NN) is a simple yet powerful classification algorithm that works by finding the **k** closest data points to a new point and assigning the most common class among those neighbors as the predicted class. The proximity between points is usually measured using distance metrics like Euclidean distance.

The core idea is that similar data points tend to have similar labels, so we classify a new point based on its similarity to known data points.

How k-NN Works

1. **Choose a value for k**: This determines how many neighbors to consider when making a prediction.

2. **Calculate the distance**: Measure the distance between the new data point and all other points in the training set.

3. **Sort the distances**: Sort the distances in ascending order and pick the top **k** closest data points.

4. **Assign the class**: Assign the class that is most common among the **k** neighbors.

The value of **k** significantly affects the model's performance. A small value of **k** can make the model sensitive to noise, while a large value can make the model too general and less sensitive to important distinctions.

Fitting a k-NN Model in R

R has several packages for implementing k-NN, such as the class package. The function knn() is used to fit a k-NN model.

Step 1: Prepare the Data

We'll use the same customer churn dataset but split it into a training and test set.

r

```r
# Load the required library
library(class)

# Sample dataset for customer churn
customer_data <- data.frame(
  Age = c(25, 30, 35, 40, 45, 50),
  Income = c(40000, 50000, 60000, 70000, 80000,
90000),
  Churn = c(0, 0, 1, 0, 1, 1)
)

# Split the data into training and test sets
set.seed(123)
train_indices <- sample(1:nrow(customer_data), size
= 0.7 * nrow(customer_data))
train_data <- customer_data[train_indices, ]
test_data <- customer_data[-train_indices, ]

# Prepare the input data (excluding the target
variable)
train_x <- train_data[, c("Age", "Income")]
test_x <- test_data[, c("Age", "Income")]
train_y <- train_data$Churn
```

test_y <- test_data$Churn

Step 2: Fit the k-NN Model

Now, let's fit the k-NN model to the training data.

r

```
# Fit the k-NN model with k = 3

knn_pred <- knn(train = train_x, test = test_x, cl = train_y, k = 3)


# Evaluate the model using a confusion matrix

table(Predicted = knn_pred, Actual = test_y)
```

The knn() function classifies the test data based on the closest neighbors in the training set. By using a confusion matrix, we can compare the predicted values with the actual values and evaluate the performance of the model.

Real-World Example: Predicting Customer Churn Using Classification

In this section, we will predict customer churn (whether a customer will leave a service or not) using classification algorithms. The goal is to identify customers at risk of churn so that retention strategies can be implemented.

Step 1: Prepare the Data

For this example, assume we have customer data with the following features: **Age, Income, Tenure**, and a target variable **Churn**, where 1 represents churn (customer left) and 0 represents no churn (customer retained).

r

```r
# Example customer churn dataset
churn_data <- data.frame(
  Age = c(30, 45, 50, 35, 60, 29),
  Income = c(45000, 65000, 70000, 55000, 80000, 40000),
  Tenure = c(5, 3, 10, 6, 2, 8),
  Churn = c(1, 0, 0, 1, 0, 1)
)
```

Step 2: Build the Decision Tree Model

We'll first build a decision tree to predict churn.

r

```r
# Fit a decision tree model
```

```
churn_tree <- rpart(Churn ~ Age + Income + Tenure,
data = churn_data, method = "class")
```

Visualize the decision tree

```
rpart.plot(churn_tree)
```

Step 3: Build the k-NN Model

Next, let's build a k-NN model to predict churn.

r

Split the data into training and test sets

```
set.seed(123)

train_indices <- sample(1:nrow(churn_data), size =
0.7 * nrow(churn_data))

train_data <- churn_data[train_indices, ]

test_data <- churn_data[-train_indices, ]
```

Fit the k-NN model with k = 3

```
knn_pred <- knn(train = train_data[, c("Age",
"Income", "Tenure")],

        test = test_data[, c("Age", "Income",
"Tenure")],

        cl = train_data$Churn, k = 3)
```

Evaluate the k-NN model using a confusion matrix

table(Predicted = knn_pred, Actual =
test_data$Churn)

Step 4: Model Evaluation

We evaluate the performance of both models
(decision tree and k-NN) by using confusion matrices.
Based on the confusion matrix, we can calculate
metrics such as accuracy, precision, recall, and F1-
score, which will guide us in choosing the best model
for predicting customer churn.

In this chapter, we explored the process of building
classification models using **Decision Trees** and **k-
Nearest Neighbors (k-NN)**. These algorithms are
powerful tools for tackling classification problems in
real-world applications like customer churn prediction.
We also discussed model evaluation techniques,
including confusion matrices, to assess the
performance of the models.

Chapter 9: Regression Models for Predictive Analytics

Introduction to Regression Models

Regression is a fundamental technique in statistical modeling and machine learning, used for predicting continuous outcomes based on one or more predictor variables. Unlike classification, where the goal is to predict a category, regression predicts a numeric value, such as price, temperature, or sales volume.

In this chapter, we will explore two primary types of regression models—**Linear Regression** and **Polynomial Regression**. We will also focus on assessing model performance using various metrics, such as **Root Mean Squared Error (RMSE)** and **R-squared**. Finally, we will apply these models to a real-world scenario of predicting sales forecasts for a retail business.

Why Regression Models?

Regression models are widely used for tasks like:

- **Predicting continuous values**: For example, predicting the price of a house based on its features (e.g., square footage, number of rooms).

- **Forecasting trends**: For example, predicting sales growth over time based on historical data.

- **Understanding relationships**: For example, understanding how various factors, like advertising expenditure, affect sales performance.

In the context of predictive analytics, regression models provide a valuable framework for forecasting and making data-driven decisions.

Linear Regression in R

What is Linear Regression?

Linear regression is one of the simplest and most widely used regression techniques. It models the relationship between a dependent variable (the target) and one or more independent variables (predictors) using a linear equation. In the case of a single predictor, the equation is:

$Y = \beta_0 + \beta_1 \cdot X + \epsilon$

Where:

- Y is the dependent variable (what we are predicting),

- XXX is the independent variable (the feature used for prediction),

- β_0\beta_0β_0 is the intercept,

- β_1\beta_1β_1 is the coefficient of the predictor, and

- ϵ\epsilon$\epsilon$ is the error term.

The objective of linear regression is to estimate the coefficients (β_0\beta_0β_0 and β_1\beta_1β_1) that minimize the difference between the predicted and actual values.

Fitting a Linear Regression Model in R

To perform linear regression in R, we can use the lm() function, which stands for **linear model**. Let's go through the steps of applying linear regression to a sales forecast example for a retail business.

Step 1: Prepare the Data

We will use a dataset where the dependent variable is **Sales** (the target we want to predict), and the independent variable is **Advertising Spend** (the feature used for prediction). The data represents monthly advertising spend and corresponding sales.

r

```
# Example retail sales dataset
sales_data <- data.frame(
  Advertising_Spend = c(10, 20, 30, 40, 50, 60),
```

Sales = c(12, 24, 32, 44, 55, 68)

)

View the dataset

print(sales_data)

Step 2: Fit the Linear Regression Model

Next, we fit the linear regression model to the data using the lm() function. In this case, we are modeling **Sales** as a function of **Advertising_Spend**.

r

Fit the linear regression model

sales_model <- lm(Sales ~ Advertising_Spend, data = sales_data)

View the summary of the model

summary(sales_model)

The summary() function provides valuable information about the model, such as:

- **Coefficients**: The values of β_0\beta_0β_0 and β_1\beta_1β_1, which indicate the intercept and slope of the linear equation.

- **R-squared**: A measure of how well the model explains the variability in the data. The higher the R-squared value, the better the model fits the data.

- **p-value**: A measure of the statistical significance of the coefficients. If the p-value is less than 0.05, the predictor variable is statistically significant.

Step 3: Evaluate Model Performance

Once the model is fit, we assess its performance by checking the residuals (the differences between actual and predicted values). If the residuals are randomly distributed, the model is a good fit.

r

```
# Predictions using the model

predictions <- predict(sales_model)


# Calculate residuals

residuals <- sales_data$Sales - predictions


# Plot the residuals

plot(residuals)
```

We can also evaluate the model using **R-squared** and **Root Mean Squared Error (RMSE)**.

- **R-squared**: This value indicates the proportion of variance in the dependent variable that is explained by the model. A higher R-squared value suggests a better fit.

- **RMSE**: This is a measure of how well the model's predictions match the actual data. Lower RMSE values indicate better model performance.

r

```r
# Calculate R-squared

rsq <- summary(sales_model)$r.squared

print(paste("R-squared: ", rsq))


# Calculate RMSE

rmse <- sqrt(mean(residuals^2))

print(paste("RMSE: ", rmse))
```

These metrics will give us a sense of how well our linear regression model is predicting sales.

Polynomial Regression in R

What is Polynomial Regression?

Polynomial regression extends linear regression by adding polynomial terms (higher-degree terms) of the independent variables. This allows the model to capture more complex, non-linear relationships between the independent and dependent variables. The general form of a polynomial regression equation is:

$Y=\beta_0+\beta_1 \cdot X+\beta_2 \cdot X2+\beta_3 \cdot X3+\cdots+\square Y = \beta\_0 + \beta\_1 \cdot X + \beta\_2 \cdot X^2 + \beta\_3 \cdot X^3 + \dots + \epsilon Y=\beta_0+\beta_1 \cdot X+\beta_2 \cdot X2+\beta_3 \cdot X3+\cdots+\square$

In polynomial regression, the model fits a curve to the data, rather than a straight line.

When to Use Polynomial Regression?

Polynomial regression is useful when there is a curvilinear relationship between the dependent and independent variables. For example, sales might initially increase with advertising spend but plateau after a certain point. Linear regression would not capture this behavior, whereas polynomial regression can model it more accurately.

Fitting a Polynomial Regression Model in R

Let's now extend the previous example by fitting a **polynomial regression** model to capture a non-linear relationship between **Advertising_Spend** and **Sales**.

Step 1: Fit the Polynomial Regression Model

We can add polynomial terms to our linear regression model by specifying the degree of the polynomial. For example, we will use a quadratic (second-degree) polynomial model:

r

```r
# Fit the polynomial regression model (degree 2)

poly_model <- lm(Sales ~ poly(Advertising_Spend, 2),
data = sales_data)


# View the summary of the polynomial model

summary(poly_model)
```

Step 2: Evaluate Model Performance

As with linear regression, we can evaluate the polynomial regression model using R-squared and RMSE:

r

```r
# Predictions using the polynomial model

poly_predictions <- predict(poly_model)


# Calculate residuals

poly_residuals <- sales_data$Sales - poly_predictions


# Calculate R-squared

poly_rsq <- summary(poly_model)$r.squared
```

```r
print(paste("R-squared for Polynomial Model: ",
poly_rsq))
```

```r
# Calculate RMSE
```

```r
poly_rmse <- sqrt(mean(poly_residuals^2))
```

```r
print(paste("RMSE for Polynomial Model: ",
poly_rmse))
```

The polynomial model should fit the data better if there is a curvilinear relationship between the predictors and the target variable.

Step 3: Visualize the Polynomial Regression

To better understand the fit of the polynomial regression, we can visualize the predictions against the actual data:

r

```r
# Plot the original data
```

```r
plot(sales_data$Advertising_Spend,
sales_data$Sales, main = "Sales vs Advertising
Spend",
    xlab = "Advertising Spend", ylab = "Sales", pch =
19, col = "blue")
```

```r
# Add the polynomial regression curve
```

```r
lines(sales_data$Advertising_Spend,
poly_predictions, col = "red", lwd = 2)
```

This plot will show the original data points and the fitted polynomial regression curve.

Real-World Example: Predicting Sales Forecasts for a Retail Business

Scenario

Imagine a retail business wants to forecast sales based on monthly advertising spend. The company collects data on **Advertising Spend** and **Sales** over several months, and our task is to build a model to predict future sales based on advertising spend.

Step 1: Prepare the Data

We'll assume we have a dataset with the following columns: **Month**, **Advertising_Spend**, and **Sales**.

r

```r
# Example retail sales dataset
sales_data <- data.frame(
  Month = c("Jan", "Feb", "Mar", "Apr", "May", "Jun"),
  Advertising_Spend = c(5000, 7000, 8000, 9000, 10000, 11000),
```

```
  Sales = c(12000, 15000, 18000, 21000, 24000,
27000)
)
```

View the dataset

print(sales_data)

Step 2: Fit Linear and Polynomial Models

We will fit both a linear and polynomial regression model to the sales data and compare their performance.

r

Linear model

```
linear_model <- lm(Sales ~ Advertising_Spend, data =
sales_data)
```

Polynomial model (degree 2)

```
poly_model <- lm(Sales ~ poly(Advertising_Spend, 2),
data = sales_data)
```

Step 3: Evaluate Models

We will evaluate both models using **R-squared** and **RMSE**.

r

```r
# Evaluate the linear model

linear_rsq <- summary(linear_model)$r.squared

linear_rmse <- sqrt(mean((sales_data$Sales -
predict(linear_model))^2))


# Evaluate the polynomial model

poly_rsq <- summary(poly_model)$r.squared

poly_rmse <- sqrt(mean((sales_data$Sales -
predict(poly_model))^2))
```

Step 4: Make Predictions

Finally, we use the best-performing model (based on R-squared and RMSE) to make predictions for future months.

r

```r
# Predict future sales using the best model

future_advertising_spend <- c(12000, 13000, 14000)

predictions <- predict(poly_model, newdata =
data.frame(Advertising_Spend =
future_advertising_spend))
```

In this chapter, we explored **linear regression** and **polynomial regression** models in R, focusing on their application for predictive analytics. We discussed how to fit and evaluate both models, assess performance using metrics like **R-squared** and **RMSE**, and apply these techniques to a real-world sales forecasting problem.

Understanding regression models is essential for making data-driven decisions in business and data science. Whether you're predicting sales, estimating costs, or forecasting trends, regression provides a powerful tool for modeling relationships between variables and making accurate predictions.

Chapter 10: Machine Learning with Random Forests and SVM

Introduction to Machine Learning Models

In the realm of machine learning, two powerful algorithms that have gained widespread use are **Random Forests** and **Support Vector Machines (SVM)**. Both are supervised learning techniques used for classification and regression tasks, with unique strengths and areas of application. In this chapter, we will explore these algorithms in depth, learn how to implement them in R, and apply them to a real-world example: predicting loan defaults.

We will also use the **caret** package, an incredibly powerful and user-friendly tool in R for streamlining the implementation of machine learning models, to handle the complexities of training, tuning, and evaluating these models.

Overview of Random Forests

What is a Random Forest?

A **Random Forest** is an ensemble learning algorithm that creates a collection of decision trees and combines their results to improve accuracy and reduce overfitting. It is a type of **bagging** method, where each individual tree is built on a random subset of the data and features. The predictions of the trees are then aggregated, typically by majority vote in the case of classification tasks, or averaging in regression tasks.

The key benefits of Random Forests include:

- **Improved accuracy**: By aggregating multiple decision trees, Random Forests are less likely to overfit compared to individual decision trees.

- **Handling large datasets**: Random Forests can handle both classification and regression tasks efficiently, even with large datasets.

- **Feature importance**: Random Forests can provide valuable insights into which features contribute most to the prediction.

Working of Random Forest

1. **Bootstrap sampling**: Multiple subsets of the dataset are generated by sampling with replacement. Each decision tree is trained on a different subset of the data.

2. **Feature randomization**: Each tree is trained using a random subset of the available features, ensuring that the trees are not highly correlated.

3. **Aggregation**: For classification tasks, the final prediction is made by taking a majority vote from all the trees; for regression tasks, the final

prediction is the average of the individual tree predictions.

Advantages of Random Forest

- **Robust to overfitting**: Random Forests reduce overfitting by averaging the results of multiple trees, each trained on different subsets of data.

- **Handles missing values well**: Random Forests can handle missing values in both the training data and test data without needing imputation.

Overview of Support Vector Machines (SVM)

What is an SVM?

Support Vector Machines (SVMs) are supervised learning algorithms used for classification and regression tasks. The core idea behind SVM is to find a hyperplane that best separates data points of different classes. SVMs are particularly powerful for high-dimensional data and have become one of the go-to algorithms for classification problems.

Working of SVM

1. **Hyperplane**: SVM tries to find a hyperplane (a decision boundary) that separates the classes in the best possible way. For a binary classification problem, this would be a line (in

two dimensions), a plane (in three dimensions), or a higher-dimensional hyperplane.

2. **Maximizing the margin**: SVM maximizes the margin between the two classes, which is the distance from the nearest data point of each class to the hyperplane. This margin maximization helps in generalizing the model to new, unseen data.

3. **Support Vectors**: The data points that are closest to the hyperplane are called **support vectors**. These points are crucial for defining the position and orientation of the hyperplane.

Types of SVM

- **Linear SVM**: Used when the data is linearly separable, i.e., the classes can be separated by a straight line (or hyperplane).

- **Non-linear SVM**: When the data is not linearly separable, the kernel trick is used to transform the data into a higher-dimensional space where it becomes linearly separable.

Advantages of SVM

- **Effective in high-dimensional spaces**: SVM is highly effective in cases where the number of features is large compared to the number of data points.

- **Versatility**: SVM can be used for both linear and non-linear classification problems.

Implementing Random Forest and SVM in R

Both **Random Forest** and **SVM** can be easily implemented in R using the **caret** package, which provides a consistent interface for training and evaluating machine learning models. Let's walk through the steps of using **caret** to build and evaluate both models.

Step 1: Installing and Loading Necessary Packages

Before we begin, we need to install and load the required packages. The **caret** package will help us train, tune, and evaluate both Random Forest and SVM models, while the **randomForest** and **e1071** packages will provide the implementations of these algorithms.

r

```
# Install the caret package and required dependencies

install.packages("caret")

install.packages("randomForest")

install.packages("e1071")


# Load the libraries

library(caret)
```

```r
library(randomForest)

library(e1071)
```

Step 2: Preparing the Data

For this chapter, we'll use a dataset of **loan applicants**. The goal is to predict whether a loan applicant will default on their loan. The dataset includes various features such as age, income, loan amount, and other factors that might influence the likelihood of default.

r

```r
# Example loan default dataset

loan_data <- read.csv("loan_data.csv")


# View the first few rows of the dataset

head(loan_data)


# Split the dataset into training and test sets (70% for training, 30% for testing)

set.seed(123)

train_index <- createDataPartition(loan_data$Default, p = 0.7, list = FALSE)

train_data <- loan_data[train_index, ]

test_data <- loan_data[-train_index, ]
```

Step 3: Training a Random Forest Model

We will first train a **Random Forest** model to predict loan defaults. Using the **caret** package, we can easily train the model using the train() function.

r

```
# Train the Random Forest model using caret
rf_model <- train(Default ~ ., data = train_data, method = "rf", trControl = trainControl(method = "cv"))
```

```
# View the model details
print(rf_model)
```

Step 4: Training an SVM Model

Next, we will train a **Support Vector Machine (SVM)** model using the same training data. For classification tasks, we will use the svm() method from the **e1071** package.

r

```
# Train the SVM model using caret
svm_model <- train(Default ~ ., data = train_data, method = "svmRadial", trControl = trainControl(method = "cv"))
```

```
# View the model details
```

```
print(svm_model)
```

Step 5: Evaluating Model Performance

After training the models, we can evaluate their performance on the test data using various metrics such as accuracy, precision, recall, and the confusion matrix. We can also compare both models to determine which performs better.

Step 5.1: Random Forest Evaluation

r

```
# Predict using the Random Forest model

rf_predictions <- predict(rf_model, newdata = test_data)


# Confusion matrix for the Random Forest model

confusionMatrix(rf_predictions, test_data$Default)
```

Step 5.2: SVM Evaluation

r

```
# Predict using the SVM model

svm_predictions <- predict(svm_model, newdata = test_data)


# Confusion matrix for the SVM model
```

```
confusionMatrix(svm_predictions, test_data$Default)
```

The confusion matrix provides a detailed breakdown of the model's performance, including metrics such as:

- **Accuracy**: The proportion of correct predictions (both true positives and true negatives).

- **Precision**: The proportion of positive predictions that were actually correct.

- **Recall**: The proportion of actual positives that were correctly predicted.

- **F1-score**: A balance between precision and recall.

Real-World Example: Predicting Loan Defaults

Scenario

Imagine a bank wants to predict whether a loan applicant will default on their loan. The bank uses a variety of features, including **income**, **age**, **loan amount**, and **credit score**, to make this prediction.

The goal is to build a machine learning model that can predict the likelihood of loan defaults based on these features. In this chapter, we used both **Random Forest** and **Support Vector Machines (SVM)** to model the relationship between these features and loan defaults.

Step 1: Data Preparation

We started by loading the loan dataset, splitting it into training and testing sets, and exploring the features of the data. This step is crucial for understanding the data and ensuring that we have enough information to train our models effectively.

Step 2: Model Training

Using **Random Forest** and **SVM**, we trained two models on the training data. Both algorithms have their strengths.

- **Random Forest** handles large datasets and provides a robust, ensemble-based approach to classification.

- **SVM** is effective in high-dimensional spaces and is particularly useful when the classes are not linearly separable.

Step 3: Model Evaluation

After training the models, we evaluated their performance using a confusion matrix. This allowed us to assess the accuracy, precision, recall, and F1-score of each model. Depending on the results, we could choose the best model for predicting loan defaults.

In this chapter, we explored two powerful machine learning algorithms: **Random Forest** and **Support**

Vector Machines (SVM). We implemented these models in R using the **caret** package and applied them to a real-world problem of predicting loan defaults. By comparing the models' performance, we can choose the best model to support the bank's decision-making process.

Chapter 11: Neural Networks and Deep Learning with R

Introduction to Neural Networks and Deep Learning Concepts

In recent years, **Neural Networks** and **Deep Learning** have revolutionized the field of data science and machine learning. From image recognition to natural language processing, deep learning models have achieved state-of-the-art results across various domains. These models, inspired by the human brain's architecture, are capable of learning complex patterns and representations from large datasets.

In this chapter, we will explore the basic concepts of neural networks and deep learning, delve into how to build neural networks using the **keras** package in R, and apply them to a **real-world image classification** task. We will cover the following key concepts:

1. **What are Neural Networks?**

2. **Introduction to Deep Learning**

3. **Components of a Neural Network**

4. **Building and Training Neural Networks in R with Keras**

What are Neural Networks?

At a high level, a **neural network** is a computational model that attempts to simulate how the human brain processes information. Neural networks consist of layers of interconnected nodes (or neurons), each performing simple computations. These networks are used to detect patterns in data and make predictions based on those patterns.

A **neuron** in a neural network is similar to a biological neuron in the human brain. It takes one or more inputs, processes them through an activation function, and produces an output. These outputs can then serve as the inputs for subsequent neurons in deeper layers.

Basic Neural Network Structure

A typical neural network consists of three main types of layers:

1. **Input Layer**: The layer that takes in the data. Each node represents a feature of the dataset.

2. **Hidden Layers**: One or more intermediate layers where computations and transformations happen. Each hidden layer contains multiple neurons.

3. **Output Layer**: The final layer that provides the predictions or classifications based on the inputs and transformations from the previous layers.

These layers are connected by **weights**, which determine the strength of the connections between neurons. The goal of training a neural network is to adjust these weights to minimize the error between the predicted outputs and the true labels in the data.

Introduction to Deep Learning

Deep learning is a subset of machine learning that deals with neural networks having multiple hidden layers. These multi-layered models are known as **deep neural networks (DNNs)**. Deep learning enables the model to learn highly complex patterns and hierarchical representations from large datasets, making it extremely effective for tasks like **image recognition**, **speech recognition**, and **natural language processing**.

The main difference between traditional machine learning and deep learning is the level of abstraction. While traditional algorithms often require feature engineering (manual selection and transformation of features), deep learning models can automatically learn the best features directly from raw data, such as pixels in images or raw text.

Deep learning has gained popularity in recent years due to the increase in computational power and the availability of large datasets.

Components of a Neural Network

1. Neurons and Weights

A neural network is composed of **neurons**, each connected to other neurons via **weights**. The neurons take input data, apply an activation function, and produce output. The weights are adjusted during training to minimize the prediction error.

2. Activation Functions

Activation functions define the output of a neuron given a certain input. They introduce **non-linearity** to the network, allowing it to learn complex relationships between the data. Common activation functions include:

- **Sigmoid**: Squashes the output between 0 and 1, used mainly for binary classification tasks.

- **ReLU (Rectified Linear Unit)**: Provides faster training and allows the network to handle more complex patterns.

- **Softmax**: Used in the output layer for multi-class classification tasks, normalizing the output into probabilities.

3. Loss Function

The loss function measures how well the neural network's predictions match the true labels in the dataset. Common loss functions include:

- **Mean Squared Error (MSE)**: Used for regression tasks.

- **Cross-Entropy Loss**: Used for classification tasks, comparing the predicted probabilities with the true class labels.

4. Optimization

Optimization algorithms, like **gradient descent**, are used to adjust the weights of the neural network to minimize the loss function. The weights are updated iteratively based on the gradients of the loss function with respect to the weights.

Building and Training Neural Networks in R with Keras

The **keras** package in R provides an interface to the **Keras** library, which is a high-level neural network API running on top of other deep learning frameworks, such as **TensorFlow**. Keras is widely used for building and training deep learning models due to its simplicity and flexibility.

To get started with Keras in R, we first need to install the necessary packages.

r

```
# Install necessary packages

install.packages("keras")

library(keras)


# Install TensorFlow backend (required for Keras to
work)

install_keras()
```

After installation, we can start building a neural
network model. Keras provides a simple interface for
adding layers, specifying activation functions, and
defining the architecture of the network.

Example: Building a Neural Network for Image Classification

Let's walk through a practical example of building a
basic neural network for image classification using the
Fashion MNIST dataset. This dataset consists of
images of clothing items (e.g., shirts, trousers, etc.)
and is commonly used for benchmarking image
classification models.

1. **Load the Dataset**

We will begin by loading the Fashion MNIST dataset,
which is available directly in Keras. This dataset

consists of 60,000 training images and 10,000 test images.

r

```r
# Load the Fashion MNIST dataset
fashion_mnist <- dataset_fashion_mnist()

# Split the data into training and testing sets
train_images <- fashion_mnist$train$x
train_labels <- fashion_mnist$train$y
test_images <- fashion_mnist$test$x
test_labels <- fashion_mnist$test$y

# Normalize the image data to values between 0 and 1
train_images <- train_images / 255
test_images <- test_images / 255
```

2. **Preprocess the Data**

Before feeding the images into the neural network, we need to preprocess the data. This includes flattening the images into vectors and one-hot encoding the labels for classification.

r

```r
# Flatten the images from 28x28 to a 784-dimensional vector

train_images <- array_reshape(train_images, c(nrow(train_images), 784))

test_images <- array_reshape(test_images, c(nrow(test_images), 784))


# One-hot encode the labels

train_labels <- to_categorical(train_labels, 10)

test_labels <- to_categorical(test_labels, 10)
```

3. **Build the Neural Network Model**

Now, we can define the architecture of the neural network. For this task, we will use a **fully connected feedforward network** with one hidden layer.

r

```r
# Build the model

model <- keras_model_sequential() %>%

  layer_dense(units = 128, activation = "relu", input_shape = c(784)) %>%

  layer_dense(units = 10, activation = "softmax")


# Compile the model

model %>% compile(
```

```
loss = "categorical_crossentropy",

optimizer = optimizer_adam(),

metrics = c("accuracy")
)
```

In this example, the neural network consists of:

- An **input layer** of 784 units (one for each pixel in the 28x28 image).

- A **hidden layer** with 128 units and ReLU activation.

- An **output layer** with 10 units (one for each clothing class), using the **softmax** activation to output probabilities.

4. **Train the Model**

We can now train the model using the training data.

r


```
# Train the model
model %>% fit(train_images, train_labels, epochs = 5, batch_size = 128)
```

In this example, we train the model for 5 epochs, adjusting the weights to minimize the loss function using the **Adam optimizer**.

5. **Evaluate the Model**

Once the model is trained, we can evaluate its performance on the test dataset.

r

```
# Evaluate the model on the test data

score <- model %>% evaluate(test_images,
test_labels)


cat("Test loss:", score$loss, "\n")

cat("Test accuracy:", score$accuracy, "\n")
```

This will output the **loss** and **accuracy** of the model on the test data. Typically, a well-trained neural network will achieve an accuracy of over 90% on the Fashion MNIST dataset.

Real-World Example: Image Classification Using a Neural Network

In this real-world example, we used a neural network to classify images from the **Fashion MNIST** dataset. This dataset, though small and simple, is a great starting point for learning the fundamentals of deep learning and neural networks.

Key Steps:

1. **Data Loading and Preprocessing**: We loaded the image dataset, normalized the pixel values,

and reshaped the images for the neural network.

2. **Building the Neural Network**: We defined a simple feedforward neural network with one hidden layer and an output layer for classification.

3. **Training the Model**: We trained the neural network on the training data using the Adam optimizer and categorical cross-entropy loss.

4. **Evaluating the Model**: We evaluated the model on the test dataset, measuring its accuracy in classifying the images.

This process can be adapted for more complex datasets, such as those used in medical image analysis, autonomous driving, or even video surveillance.

In this chapter, we explored the basics of **neural networks** and **deep learning**. We built a basic neural network using the **keras** package in R and applied it to an image classification problem with the Fashion MNIST dataset. Neural networks are a powerful tool for solving complex problems, and with deep learning frameworks like Keras, you can easily build, train, and evaluate these models in R. As you advance, you can explore more complex architectures and apply deep learning to more sophisticated tasks.

Chapter 12: Model Evaluation and Hyperparameter Tuning

Introduction

In the previous chapters, we have covered a variety of machine learning models and techniques for building and training them. However, building a model is just the first step in the data science pipeline. To ensure the reliability and robustness of the model's predictions, it is crucial to evaluate its performance. Furthermore, the performance of machine learning models can often be improved through **hyperparameter tuning**—the process of optimizing model parameters to achieve better accuracy.

In this chapter, we will explore the following key concepts:

1. **Model Evaluation**: Techniques for assessing the effectiveness of a model, including cross-validation and confusion matrices.

2. **Hyperparameter Tuning**: Approaches for fine-tuning model parameters, particularly using **grid search** to find the optimal set of hyperparameters.

3. **Real-World Example**: We will apply these techniques to a classification task of **email spam detection**, where we will evaluate and tune a model to improve its performance.

---

1. Model Evaluation Techniques

Model evaluation is the process of assessing how well a model performs based on some predefined criteria, typically involving metrics such as **accuracy**, **precision**, **recall**, **F1 score**, and others. Evaluating a model properly ensures that the model is making the right predictions and is not overfitting or underfitting the data.

1.1 Cross-Validation

One of the most important techniques for model evaluation is **cross-validation**, which helps in understanding how well the model generalizes to unseen data. It is commonly used to avoid the problem of overfitting (where the model performs well on the training set but poorly on unseen data).

Cross-validation involves splitting the data into multiple subsets (or "folds") and training the model on different combinations of these subsets. In a typical cross-validation setup, the dataset is divided into **k** folds. The model is trained on **k-1** folds and tested on the remaining fold. This process is repeated **k** times, each time using a different fold as the test set.

The most commonly used type of cross-validation is **k-fold cross-validation**, where the dataset is divided into **k** equal folds, and the model is trained and tested **k** times. The final evaluation metric is the average of the individual evaluations from each fold.

Here's an example of how to perform **k-fold cross-validation** in R using the **caret** package:

r

```
# Load the caret package for cross-validation

library(caret)


# Define a 10-fold cross-validation

train_control <- trainControl(method = "cv", number = 10)


# Define a model (e.g., Random Forest)

model <- train(target ~ ., data = dataset, method = "rf", trControl = train_control)


# View the model's performance

print(model)
```

In this example, the **trainControl** function is used to specify the cross-validation method (10-fold in this case), and the **train** function from the caret package is used to train the Random Forest model. The **trControl** argument specifies the cross-validation method.

1.2 Confusion Matrix

Another essential tool for model evaluation is the **confusion matrix**, which provides a detailed summary of how well the classification model is performing. A confusion matrix compares the predicted labels with the true labels and gives a breakdown of the model's correct and incorrect predictions.

For a binary classification task (e.g., spam vs. non-spam), a confusion matrix looks like this:

	Predicted No	**Predicted Yes**
Actual No	True Negative (TN)	False Positive (FP)
Actual Yes	False Negative (FN)	True Positive (TP)

The confusion matrix allows us to compute several important evaluation metrics:

- **Accuracy**: The percentage of correct predictions (both true positives and true negatives) out of all predictions.

Accuracy=TP+TNTP+TN+FP+FNAccuracy = \frac{TP + TN}{TP + TN + FP + FN}Accuracy=TP+TN+FP+FNTP+TN

- **Precision**: The percentage of true positives among all predicted positives.

$$Precision = \frac{TP}{TP + FP}$$

- **Recall (Sensitivity)**: The percentage of true positives among all actual positives.

$$Recall = \frac{TP}{TP + FN}$$

- **F1 Score**: The harmonic mean of precision and recall, which is especially useful when dealing with imbalanced datasets.

$$F1 = 2 \times \frac{Precision \times Recall}{Precision + Recall}$$

In R, the confusion matrix can be generated using the **caret** or **e1071** packages:

r

```
# Generate confusion matrix

confusionMatrix(predictions, actual_labels)
```

This will give you not only the confusion matrix itself but also metrics such as accuracy, precision, recall, and F1 score.

---

2. Hyperparameter Tuning

While training a model, we typically choose certain **hyperparameters** that influence its performance. For example, in decision trees, hyperparameters such as **max_depth**, **min_samples_split**, and **min_samples_leaf** control the tree's complexity. Similarly, for algorithms like **Random Forests** or **Support Vector Machines (SVM)**, hyperparameters such as the number of trees (in Random Forests) or the kernel type (in SVM) can significantly impact model performance.

Hyperparameter tuning is the process of systematically searching for the best set of hyperparameters that optimize model performance. There are two common approaches for hyperparameter tuning:

2.1 Grid Search

Grid search is a brute-force approach where a set of hyperparameters is defined, and the model is trained and evaluated for every possible combination of these hyperparameters. For example, if we want to tune the **C** parameter of an SVM and the **kernel** type, a grid search would evaluate all combinations of values for these parameters.

Here's how you can implement **grid search** in R using the **caret** package:

r

```
# Define the hyperparameters grid
grid <- expand.grid(.mtry = c(1, 2, 3, 4), .ntree = c(50, 100, 200))
```

```
# Set up cross-validation

train_control <- trainControl(method = "cv", number =
10)


# Apply grid search for a Random Forest model

model <- train(target ~ ., data = dataset, method =
"rf", trControl = train_control, tuneGrid = grid)


# View the results

print(model)
```

In this example:

- We specify a grid of values for **mtry** (number of variables randomly sampled at each split) and **ntree** (number of trees in the forest).

- We use 10-fold cross-validation and perform the grid search over all combinations of the hyperparameters.

2.2 Random Search

In contrast to grid search, **random search** randomly samples hyperparameters from a predefined distribution. It can be more efficient than grid search, especially when dealing with a large number of hyperparameters.

Here's an example of using **random search** in R:

r

Define the hyperparameters range for random search

```
grid_random <- expand.grid(.mtry = sample(1:5, 10, replace = TRUE),
                    .ntree = sample(50:200, 10, replace = TRUE))
```

Train the model using random search

```
model <- train(target ~ ., data = dataset, method = "rf", trControl = train_control, tuneGrid = grid_random)
```

View the results

```
print(model)
```

In this case, we use sample() to generate random values for **mtry** and **ntree** and perform random search.

---

3. Real-World Example: Tuning a Classification Model for Email Spam Detection

Let's now apply these techniques to a **real-world classification task**: predicting whether an email is

spam or **not spam**. The goal is to build and evaluate a classification model and then use hyperparameter tuning to optimize it.

3.1 Dataset: Email Spam Detection

The **SMS Spam Collection** dataset is commonly used for spam detection tasks. The dataset contains a collection of SMS messages labeled as either spam or ham (non-spam). We will use this dataset to build a classification model.

First, load the necessary libraries and dataset:

r

```
# Load required libraries

library(caret)

library(tm)

library(randomForest)


# Load the dataset (assuming it's in a CSV file)

spam_data <- read.csv("sms_spam_collection.csv")


# Preprocess the text data (convert to lowercase,
remove stop words, etc.)

spam_data$text <- tolower(spam_data$text)

spam_data$text <-
removePunctuation(spam_data$text)
```

```r
spam_data$text <- removeNumbers(spam_data$text)

spam_data$text <- stripWhitespace(spam_data$text)
```

3.2 Feature Extraction

Next, we extract features from the text data. A common approach is to use **Bag of Words** or **TF-IDF** (Term Frequency-Inverse Document Frequency) to represent the text.

r

```r
# Create a Document-Term Matrix (DTM)

corpus <- Corpus(VectorSource(spam_data$text))

dtm <- DocumentTermMatrix(corpus)
```

3.3 Model Training and Evaluation

We will train a **Random Forest** model to classify the emails and evaluate its performance using cross-validation and confusion matrix.

r

```r
# Train the model with cross-validation

train_control <- trainControl(method = "cv", number = 10)

model_rf <- train(label ~ ., data = spam_data, method = "rf", trControl = train_control)
```

```
# Evaluate the model
```

```
confusionMatrix(model_rf)
```

3.4 Hyperparameter Tuning

Finally, we will use **grid search** to tune the hyperparameters of the Random Forest model.

r

```
# Define the hyperparameter grid
```

```
grid <- expand.grid(.mtry = c(1, 2, 3, 4), .ntree = c(50, 100, 200))
```

```
# Perform grid search
```

```
tuned_model <- train(label ~ ., data = spam_data,
method = "rf", trControl = train_control, tuneGrid =
grid)
```

```
# View the best tuned model
```

```
print(tuned_model)
```

3.5 Conclusion

In this example, we applied the concepts of model evaluation and hyperparameter tuning to a spam detection task. We used **cross-validation** to evaluate the model's performance and then applied **grid search** to find the optimal hyperparameters for the Random Forest model.

In this chapter, we learned the importance of **model evaluation** and **hyperparameter tuning** in building robust machine learning models. We explored various evaluation techniques such as **cross-validation** and the **confusion matrix**, as well as hyperparameter tuning methods like **grid search** and **random search**. Through the example of **email spam detection**, we saw how to implement these techniques in practice.

Chapter 13: Time Series Forecasting with R

Introduction to Time Series Analysis

Time series analysis is a critical component in data science and predictive analytics. It is used to analyze data points collected or recorded at specific time intervals, often to identify trends, seasonal patterns, and cyclical behavior. The goal is to model this historical data to forecast future values, which is particularly useful in fields like finance, economics, supply chain management, and demand forecasting.

In this chapter, we will explore time series analysis and forecasting using R. Specifically, we will cover:

1. **Introduction to Time Series**: Understanding the basics of time series data, its components, and common patterns.

2. **Forecasting Models**: We will explore popular time series forecasting methods like ARIMA (AutoRegressive Integrated Moving Average), Exponential Smoothing, and Prophet.

3. **Real-World Example**: We will apply these methods to forecast demand for a product over time.

By the end of this chapter, you will be equipped to use R to perform time series forecasting, analyze trends, and make data-driven predictions.

---

1. What is Time Series Data?

Time series data consists of a sequence of data points ordered in time. Each data point typically corresponds to a specific timestamp, and the key feature of time series data is its temporal order. In time series analysis, we treat time as a continuous variable, and the observations are assumed to be dependent on time.

1.1 Components of Time Series

A time series is usually decomposed into four main components:

1. **Trend**: The long-term movement or direction in the data. For example, the rising demand for a product over several years is a trend.

2. **Seasonality**: The regular, repeating fluctuations in the data over a fixed period. This could be daily, weekly, or annual patterns, such as increased retail sales during the holiday season.

3. **Cyclicality**: Similar to seasonality, but with less predictable periods. Cycles can be long-term fluctuations such as economic booms and recessions.

4. **Noise**: The random variation in data that cannot be attributed to trend, seasonality, or cyclicality.

1.2 Time Series Patterns

The first step in analyzing time series data is to visualize it and understand the underlying patterns. This can be done using basic plots in R, such as the time series plot (line plot) and decomposition plots.

2. Time Series Forecasting Models

Time series forecasting involves building a model to predict future values based on past data. Several techniques are used in time series forecasting, and we will discuss three popular ones in R: **ARIMA**, **Exponential Smoothing**, and **Prophet**.

2.1 ARIMA (AutoRegressive Integrated Moving Average)

ARIMA is one of the most commonly used models for time series forecasting. It combines three components:

1. **AR (AutoRegressive)**: The model uses past values of the time series to predict future values. The order of the AR component, denoted as p, indicates how many lag observations are used.

2. **I (Integrated)**: This component is responsible for making the time series stationary by

differencing the data. The order of differencing is denoted by d.

3. **MA (Moving Average)**: The model uses past forecast errors to predict future values. The order of the MA component, denoted by q, determines how many previous forecast errors are used.

The ARIMA model is often written as ARIMA(p, d, q), where:

- **p**: The number of lag observations included in the model (AR term).

- **d**: The number of times the data has been differenced to achieve stationarity (I term).

- **q**: The number of past forecast errors in the model (MA term).

To build an ARIMA model in R, you can use the **forecast** package. Here's a step-by-step approach:

r

```
# Install and load the forecast package

install.packages("forecast")

library(forecast)


# Load your time series data (e.g., product demand over time)
```

```r
data <- ts(your_data, frequency = 12)  # Frequency =
12 for monthly data


# Fit an ARIMA model

arima_model <- auto.arima(data)


# Forecast the next 12 periods

forecast_data <- forecast(arima_model, h = 12)


# Plot the forecast

plot(forecast_data)
```

In this example, the auto.arima() function automatically selects the best ARIMA model based on the AIC (Akaike Information Criterion). The forecast() function generates future predictions, and plot() visualizes the forecast.

2.2 Exponential Smoothing

Exponential Smoothing models are simple yet effective time series forecasting methods. They give more weight to recent observations and less weight to older observations. Exponential smoothing is ideal when there are no strong trends or seasonal patterns, but it can also be extended to capture both.

The most common forms of Exponential Smoothing are:

1. **Simple Exponential Smoothing**: Used for time series data without trend or seasonality.

2. **Holt's Linear Trend Model**: Extends simple exponential smoothing to capture linear trends.

3. **Holt-Winters' Seasonal Model**: Extends Holt's method to capture both trends and seasonality.

The **Holt-Winters** model is often used for time series forecasting with both trend and seasonality. The forecast package in R provides an implementation of these methods.

Here's how to fit a Holt-Winters model:

r

```
# Fit a Holt-Winters model

holt_winters_model <- HoltWinters(data)


# Forecast the next 12 periods

forecast_hw <- forecast(holt_winters_model, h = 12)


# Plot the forecast

plot(forecast_hw)
```

This method works well for time series data that exhibit **both trend and seasonality**, such as product demand over several months.

2.3 Prophet

Prophet is a forecasting tool developed by Facebook, and it's particularly useful for time series data that exhibits strong seasonal effects, holidays, and other trends. Prophet is designed to handle missing data and outliers more effectively than traditional models like ARIMA and Exponential Smoothing.

To use Prophet in R, the prophet package is available, and it offers an easy-to-use interface. Prophet works by fitting a piecewise linear or logistic growth trend, and it accounts for seasonality, holidays, and custom events.

Here's how to use Prophet for forecasting:

r

```
# Install and load the prophet package

install.packages("prophet")

library(prophet)


# Prepare the data (Prophet requires two columns: ds and y)

df <- data.frame(ds = your_time_column, y = your_data_column)


# Fit the Prophet model
```

```
prophet_model <- prophet(df)

# Make a future dataframe for prediction
future <- make_future_dataframe(prophet_model,
periods = 12)

# Generate forecasts
forecast_prophet <- predict(prophet_model, future)

# Plot the forecast
plot(prophet_model, forecast_prophet)
```

Prophet is highly flexible and can handle complex seasonality, making it ideal for situations where you need to account for events like holidays, marketing campaigns, or significant external influences on the time series.

---

3. Real-World Example: Forecasting Demand for a Product

Now that we've covered three popular time series forecasting methods, let's apply them to a real-world example: **forecasting demand for a product** over time.

3.1 Dataset: Product Demand

Assume we have historical demand data for a product over the past two years. The data is collected monthly, and the objective is to predict future demand for the next six months.

r

```
# Load the historical demand data
demand_data <- ts(c(120, 130, 145, 160, 170, 180, 190, 210, 225, 240, 250, 260,

          270, 280, 300, 310, 320, 340, 350, 360, 380, 390, 410, 420),

          frequency = 12, start = c(2020, 1))


# Plot the demand data
plot(demand_data, main = "Product Demand Over Time", ylab = "Demand", xlab = "Time")
```

3.2 Fitting ARIMA Model

First, we will fit an ARIMA model to this demand data:

r

```
# Fit an ARIMA model
arima_model <- auto.arima(demand_data)
```

```r
# Forecast the next 6 months
forecast_arima <- forecast(arima_model, h = 6)


# Plot the forecast
plot(forecast_arima, main = "ARIMA Forecast for Product Demand")
```

3.3 Fitting Holt-Winters Model

Next, we will fit a Holt-Winters model:

r

```r
# Fit a Holt-Winters model
holt_winters_model <- HoltWinters(demand_data)


# Forecast the next 6 months
forecast_hw <- forecast(holt_winters_model, h = 6)


# Plot the forecast
plot(forecast_hw, main = "Holt-Winters Forecast for Product Demand")
```

3.4 Fitting Prophet Model

Finally, we will fit a Prophet model to the data:

r

```r
# Prepare data for Prophet
df <- data.frame(ds = seq.Date(from = as.Date("2020-
01-01"), by = "month", length.out =
length(demand_data)),

               y = demand_data)


# Fit the Prophet model
prophet_model <- prophet(df)


# Create a future dataframe
future <- make_future_dataframe(prophet_model,
periods = 6, freq = "month")


# Forecast the next 6 months
forecast_prophet <- predict(prophet_model, future)


# Plot the forecast
plot(prophet_model, forecast_prophet)
```

In this chapter, we explored time series forecasting with R. We learned how to use different forecasting techniques, including **ARIMA, Exponential Smoothing**, and **Prophet**. Each of these methods has its strengths and can be used based on the nature of the time series data at hand.

By working through a real-world example of forecasting product demand, you should now have a solid understanding of how to apply time series forecasting techniques in R. The next step is to dive deeper into more advanced forecasting models and techniques for more complex datasets.

Chapter 14: Clustering and Unsupervised Learning

Introduction to Unsupervised Learning Techniques

Unsupervised learning refers to a class of machine learning techniques where the model is not provided with labeled data. Instead, the goal is to identify patterns, structures, or relationships within the data itself. Unlike supervised learning, where the algorithm learns from input-output pairs, unsupervised learning is used when you have data without any labels or predefined outcomes.

Clustering, a core technique in unsupervised learning, is the process of grouping similar data points together. This chapter will cover clustering techniques like **K-means clustering** and **hierarchical clustering**. We will also explore a real-world example of customer segmentation based on purchase behavior.

In this chapter, we will focus on:

1. **Introduction to Unsupervised Learning**: Understanding what unsupervised learning is and why it's useful.

2. **Clustering**: A deep dive into clustering techniques such as K-means and hierarchical clustering.

3. **Real-World Example**: Segmenting customers based on purchase behavior.

By the end of this chapter, you will understand how to use unsupervised learning methods to extract valuable insights from unlabelled data, and how clustering can be applied to real-world problems like customer segmentation.

---

1. Unsupervised Learning: The Basics

Unsupervised learning is an important aspect of machine learning where the algorithm is tasked with identifying patterns or structures in the data without any explicit labels or targets. The key difference between unsupervised learning and supervised learning is that in unsupervised learning, there are no "correct" answers or labels given to the model.

The primary goal of unsupervised learning is to explore the underlying structure of the data. Some common techniques in unsupervised learning include:

- **Clustering**: Grouping similar data points together.

- **Dimensionality Reduction**: Reducing the number of features or variables in the data while retaining important information. Examples include Principal Component Analysis (PCA) and t-SNE.

- **Association Rule Learning**: Discovering relationships or associations between variables in a dataset, commonly used in market basket analysis.

Clustering is the most widely used unsupervised learning technique. It finds groups, or clusters, of similar items within the data, where items within the same cluster are more similar to each other than to those in other clusters.

2. Clustering Techniques

Clustering can be approached in various ways depending on the nature of the data and the desired outcome. Two of the most commonly used clustering methods are **K-means clustering** and **hierarchical clustering**. Let's explore these techniques in detail.

2.1 K-means Clustering

K-means clustering is a popular and simple method used to partition data into a fixed number of clusters. The algorithm works by assigning each data point to one of **K clusters** based on the similarity of the data points. The goal is to minimize the variance within each cluster.

2.1.1 Steps in K-means Clustering

1. **Initialization**: Randomly initialize **K centroids**. These centroids represent the center of each cluster.

2. **Assignment**: Assign each data point to the nearest centroid. This is usually done using a distance metric like Euclidean distance.

3. **Update**: Recalculate the centroid of each cluster by computing the mean of all the points assigned to that cluster.

4. **Repeat**. Repeat the assignment and update steps until convergence, i.e., when the centroids no longer change significantly or a specified number of iterations is reached.

2.1.2 Determining the Optimal Number of Clusters

One of the challenges with K-means clustering is choosing the right number of clusters (K). If K is too small, you may end up with overly general clusters. If K is too large, you risk overfitting the data.

To determine the optimal number of clusters, the **Elbow Method** is commonly used:

*   Plot the **within-cluster sum of squares (WCSS)** for different values of K.

*   Look for an "elbow" In the plot, where the rate of decrease in WCSS starts to slow down. The value of K at this point is considered optimal.

Here's how to implement K-means clustering in R:

r

```r
# Load the necessary library
install.packages("ggplot2")
library(ggplot2)


# Sample data: customer purchase data (e.g., two
features: annual spending and purchase frequency)
data <- data.frame(
  spending = c(500, 600, 550, 700, 850, 900, 300,
350, 400, 450, 850, 1000),
  frequency = c(5, 6, 5, 8, 9, 10, 3, 3, 4, 5, 9, 10)
)


# Use the Elbow Method to find the optimal number of
clusters
wcss <- vector()
for (i in 1:10) {
  kmeans_model <- kmeans(data, centers = i)
  wcss[i] <- kmeans_model$tot.withinss
}


# Plot WCSS to find the elbow
```

```
plot(1:10, wcss, type = 'b', main = 'Elbow Method',
xlab = 'Number of Clusters', ylab = 'WCSS')
```

```
# Fit the K-means model with the optimal number of
clusters (assume 3 clusters here)
```

```
kmeans_model <- kmeans(data, centers = 3)
```

```
# Visualize the clusters
```

```
ggplot(data, aes(x = spending, y = frequency)) +
```

```
  geom_point(aes(color =
as.factor(kmeans_model$cluster))) +
```

```
  labs(title = "K-means Clustering of Customer Data",
color = "Cluster")
```

In this example, we used K-means clustering to segment customers based on their spending and purchase frequency. The optimal number of clusters (3) was determined using the Elbow Method.

2.2 Hierarchical Clustering

Hierarchical clustering is another technique for clustering data. Unlike K-means, hierarchical clustering does not require you to specify the number of clusters in advance. Instead, it builds a tree-like structure of clusters known as a **dendrogram**, which shows the relationships between the data points and the clusters.

There are two main types of hierarchical clustering:

1. **Agglomerative Clustering**: This is a bottom-up approach, where each data point starts as its own cluster, and pairs of clusters are merged at each step based on similarity.

2. **Divisive Clustering**: This is a top-down approach, where all data points start in one cluster, and the cluster is recursively split into smaller clusters.

2.2.1 Steps in Hierarchical Clustering

1. **Compute Pairwise Distances**: Calculate the distance between every pair of data points using a distance metric (e.g., Euclidean distance).

2. **Merge Clusters**: Merge the two most similar data points or clusters into a new cluster.

3. **Repeat**: Repeat the process until all data points are in a single cluster, or until you achieve the desired number of clusters.

4. **Dendrogram**: Visualize the hierarchical structure using a dendrogram.

Here's how to implement hierarchical clustering in R:

r

```
# Compute the distance matrix
```

```
dist_matrix <- dist(data)


# Perform hierarchical clustering using agglomerative
method

hc <- hclust(dist_matrix, method = "ward.D2")


# Plot the dendrogram

plot(hc, main = "Dendrogram of Hierarchical
Clustering")


# Cut the tree to form 3 clusters

clusters <- cutree(hc, k = 3)


# Add the cluster information to the data

data$cluster <- as.factor(clusters)


# Visualize the clusters

ggplot(data, aes(x = spending, y = frequency, color =
cluster)) +

  geom_point() +

  labs(title = "Hierarchical Clustering of Customer
Data")
```

In this case, hierarchical clustering was used to segment customers based on similar characteristics, and a dendrogram was generated to visualize the relationships between the clusters.

---

3. Real-World Example: Segmenting Customers Based on Purchase Behavior

Let's now look at a real-world example where we segment customers based on their purchasing behavior. This type of segmentation can help businesses target their marketing efforts more effectively, understand customer needs, and improve product recommendations.

We'll use a dataset of customer purchase behavior, which includes features like:

- **Annual spending** (in dollars)

- **Purchase frequency** (number of purchases in a given time period)

3.1 Preparing the Data

We assume the dataset contains the following columns: CustomerID, AnnualSpending, FrequencyOfPurchases. We load this data into R and proceed with the analysis.

r

```r
# Sample customer purchase data
customer_data <- data.frame(
  CustomerID = 1:100,
  AnnualSpending = runif(100, 100, 1000),
  FrequencyOfPurchases = runif(100, 1, 15)
)


# Preview the data
head(customer_data)
```

3.2 Applying K-means Clustering

We can now apply K-means clustering to segment customers based on their annual spending and purchase frequency.

r

```r
# Use K-means clustering with 3 clusters
kmeans_result <- kmeans(customer_data[,
c("AnnualSpending", "FrequencyOfPurchases")],
centers = 3)


# Add cluster labels to the data
customer_data$Cluster <- kmeans_result$cluster
```

```
# Visualize the clusters

ggplot(customer_data, aes(x = AnnualSpending, y =
FrequencyOfPurchases, color = as.factor(Cluster))) +

  geom_point() +

  labs(title = "Customer Segmentation Based on
Purchase Behavior", color = "Cluster")
```

In this example, we have segmented customers into three distinct groups based on their purchasing behavior. Each cluster represents a different type of customer, which can be useful for tailoring marketing strategies or identifying high-value customers.

In this chapter, we covered key unsupervised learning techniques, specifically clustering methods such as **K-means clustering** and **hierarchical clustering**. We also demonstrated how to apply these techniques to real-world data, such as customer segmentation based on purchase behavior. Unsupervised learning is a powerful tool for uncovering hidden patterns in data, and clustering can be especially useful for segmenting data into meaningful groups.

Chapter 15: Natural Language Processing (NLP) in R

Introduction to Natural Language Processing (NLP)

Natural Language Processing (NLP) is a branch of artificial intelligence (AI) that focuses on enabling computers to understand, interpret, and generate human language. It is a critical component of data science and machine learning that deals with textual data. As businesses and industries increasingly generate vast amounts of textual data—be it from emails, social media posts, customer reviews, or other sources—NLP has become a powerful tool for analyzing and deriving insights from such unstructured data.

NLP is used in various applications, such as sentiment analysis, text summarization, language translation, and speech recognition. In this chapter, we will dive into the basics of NLP and text mining using R, one of the most popular programming languages for data science. We will also explore a real-world example of sentiment analysis by analyzing social media posts to gauge brand sentiment.

By the end of this chapter, you will have a comprehensive understanding of how to process text data, perform sentiment analysis, and apply NLP techniques to analyze real-world textual data.

---

1. Basics of NLP and Text Mining in R

1.1 What is NLP?

Natural Language Processing encompasses a variety of tasks related to the interaction between computers and human language. NLP techniques aim to allow machines to process and understand the nuances of human language, including syntax, semantics, and context. In practical terms, NLP allows machines to interpret raw text data in a structured manner so that it can be analyzed for insights.

Key tasks in NLP include:

- **Tokenization**: Breaking down a text into smaller units (words, sentences, etc.).

- **Text Preprocessing**: Cleaning and preparing text data for further analysis.

- **Part-of-Speech Tagging**: Identifying the grammatical roles (noun, verb, etc.) of words.

- **Named Entity Recognition (NER)**: Extracting specific entities such as names of people, organizations, dates, etc.

- **Sentiment Analysis**: Determining the sentiment or emotional tone of a text (positive, negative, neutral).

- **Topic Modeling**: Identifying the main topics or themes in a collection of text.

1.2 Text Mining in R

Text mining refers to the process of extracting useful information and patterns from large volumes of text. In R, text mining is primarily performed using packages like **tm** (text mining) and **textclean**, among others. These packages allow you to clean and preprocess text, as well as analyze it in various ways.

The **tm** package provides functions for:

- Reading and writing text data.

- Converting text to lowercase.

- Removing stopwords (commonly used words like "the", "and", "is").

- Removing punctuation, numbers, and other unwanted characters.

- Creating a document-term matrix (DTM), which represents the frequency of terms in a collection of documents.

1.3 Key Steps in NLP

Before diving into sentiment analysis and other applications, it is essential to understand the key steps in NLP. They include:

1. **Text Acquisition**: Collecting text data from various sources like websites, social media, books, etc.

2. **Text Preprocessing**: Cleaning and formatting the text data for analysis. This includes removing unnecessary characters, correcting spelling errors, and transforming the text into a standardized format.

3. **Text Analysis**: Applying various NLP techniques such as tokenization, stemming, and sentiment analysis.

4. **Modeling and Interpretation**: Building models to understand and predict patterns in the text. This could involve classifying text into categories or predicting sentiment.

---

2. Text Preprocessing and Sentiment Analysis

2.1 Text Preprocessing

Text preprocessing is an essential step in preparing raw text for analysis. It involves cleaning the text to ensure that only the relevant parts are used in the analysis. The goal is to standardize and simplify the text data so that the machine learning or NLP model can better understand it.

Common text preprocessing techniques include:

1. **Converting to Lowercase**: This step ensures that the analysis is not case-sensitive. For instance, "Happy" and "happy" should be treated as the same word.

r

```
# Convert text to lowercase

text <- "This is an example of TEXT preprocessing"

text <- tolower(text)
```

2. **Removing Punctuation**: Punctuation marks like commas, periods, and exclamation points are usually not necessary for analysis, so they can be removed.

r

```
# Remove punctuation

library(tm)

text <- removePunctuation(text)
```

3. **Removing Numbers**: Numbers often don't carry significant meaning in text analysis unless the context specifically calls for them.

r

```
# Remove numbers

text <- removeNumbers(text)
```

4. **Removing Stopwords**: Stopwords are common words (e.g., "and", "the", "of") that do not contribute much to the meaning of the text. Removing them can improve analysis efficiency.

r

```
# Remove stopwords

text <- removeWords(text, stopwords("en"))
```

5. **Stemming**: Stemming reduces words to their root form. For example, "running" becomes "run". This helps to treat different forms of a word as the same word.

r

```
# Perform stemming

text <- stemDocument(text)
```

6. **Tokenization**: This process splits the text into smaller units such as words or sentences. Tokenization is the foundation for many NLP tasks.

r

```
# Tokenize text into words

text <- unlist(strsplit(text, " "))
```

2.2 Sentiment Analysis

Sentiment analysis is the process of determining the emotional tone or sentiment behind a piece of text. This can be classified as **positive**, **negative**, or **neutral**. Sentiment analysis is widely used for analyzing social media posts, customer reviews, and other textual data.

In R, sentiment analysis can be performed using libraries like **sentimentr** or **syuzhet**. These packages use pre-built lexicons to classify words as positive or negative based on their emotional weight.

Here is an example of performing sentiment analysis using the **sentimentr** package:

r

```
# Install and load sentimentr package

install.packages("sentimentr")

library(sentimentr)


# Sample text

text <- c("I love this product! It's amazing.", "The service was terrible. I'm so disappointed.")


# Perform sentiment analysis

sentiments <- sentiment(text)
```

```
# View results
```

sentiments

In the above example, the **sentimentr** package analyzes the polarity of the text and returns the sentiment score, indicating whether the sentiment is positive or negative.

---

3. Real-World Example: Analyzing Social Media Posts for Brand Sentiment

Let's now work through a real-world example of sentiment analysis. The goal is to analyze social media posts to determine the sentiment toward a brand. For this, we will collect a sample of social media posts about a hypothetical brand and analyze them for sentiment.

3.1 Data Collection

In practice, data can be collected using APIs from platforms like Twitter or Instagram. However, for simplicity, we will use a small set of manually curated posts.

r

```
# Sample social media posts
```

```r
social_media_posts <- c(

  "I absolutely love the new product from Brand X! It's
so amazing!",

  "Brand X's customer service is terrible. I'm never
buying from them again.",

  "The new product launch from Brand X was okay,
but it could be better.",

  "I'm a big fan of Brand X! Always delivers top-notch
quality."

)
```

3.2 Text Preprocessing

Before performing sentiment analysis, we must
preprocess the text data to clean it up.

r

```r
# Load necessary libraries

library(tm)

library(sentimentr)


# Preprocess the social media posts

clean_posts <- tolower(social_media_posts)

clean_posts <- removePunctuation(clean_posts)

clean_posts <- removeWords(clean_posts,
stopwords("en"))
```

```r
# Perform sentiment analysis

sentiment_results <- sentiment(clean_posts)


# View sentiment results

sentiment_results
```

3.3 Interpreting Sentiment

After preprocessing the text and running sentiment analysis, we can examine the results. Each post will be assigned a sentiment score, which will tell us whether the post is positive, negative, or neutral. This can help us gauge how users feel about the brand.

r

```r
# Add sentiment labels

sentiment_results$sentiment_label <-
ifelse(sentiment_results$sentiment > 0, "Positive",


ifelse(sentiment_results$sentiment < 0, "Negative",
"Neutral"))


# Display results

sentiment_results
```

The output will give us sentiment labels for each post, indicating whether the social media posts express positive, negative, or neutral sentiments.

In this chapter, we explored the fundamentals of Natural Language Processing (NLP) in R, focusing on text preprocessing and sentiment analysis. We learned how to clean and preprocess text using techniques such as tokenization, removing stopwords, and stemming. We also discussed how to use sentiment analysis to determine the em

Chapter 16: Model Deployment and APIs with R

Introduction

Once you've built and trained machine learning models using R, the next crucial step is to deploy them into production environments. Model deployment involves making the trained models available for use by other systems, applications, or users in a seamless and scalable way. It allows you to turn your data science and machine learning models into practical solutions that provide real-time predictions, automation, and insights.

In this chapter, we'll dive into the process of model deployment using R and demonstrate how to use R for creating APIs. Specifically, we will focus on using the **plumber** package to build and deploy APIs for machine learning models. This chapter will provide a real-world example of deploying a predictive model designed to predict website traffic.

By the end of this chapter, you'll be equipped with the knowledge and tools necessary to deploy your R-based machine learning models as RESTful APIs, making them available for use in production environments.

1. Deploying Models in Production Environments

1.1 What is Model Deployment?

Model deployment refers to the process of integrating a trained machine learning model into a production environment where it can serve real-time predictions or perform automated tasks. This is a critical step in the machine learning lifecycle as it allows the model to be accessed by end-users, applications, or other systems in a way that is efficient, scalable, and reliable.

Some common deployment strategies include:

- **Batch Processing**: Running predictions periodically on a set of data (e.g., daily or weekly). The model is used to generate predictions for a large dataset at once.

- **Real-Time Predictions**: Providing predictions in real time, often via a web interface or an API. The model is integrated with a system or application that makes predictions on-demand as new data is received.

- **Embedded Systems**: Deploying models within devices (e.g., IoT devices, mobile phones) where they operate autonomously and make predictions on-site.

In this chapter, we will focus on real-time deployment using APIs, as it is one of the most common and scalable ways to deploy machine learning models.

1.2 Challenges in Model Deployment

Deploying machine learning models is not without its challenges. Some common challenges include:

- **Model Compatibility**: Ensuring that the model trained in a local environment works the same way when deployed to a production environment.

- **Version Control**: Managing updates and changes to models over time, as models may need to be retrained or improved.

- **Scalability**: Ensuring that the deployed model can handle varying loads and scale efficiently.

- **Latency**: Minimizing the delay between making a prediction and receiving the result.

- **Monitoring and Maintenance**: Continuously monitoring the performance of deployed models and updating them as necessary to ensure their accuracy and reliability.

2. Using R for Creating APIs with the plumber Package

2.1 Introduction to the plumber Package

The **plumber** package in R allows you to create RESTful APIs directly from R scripts. It's an excellent tool for deploying machine learning models built in R, as it allows you to expose model predictions as API endpoints that can be accessed over the web or by other applications.

A RESTful API (Representational State Transfer) is an architectural style for designing networked applications. It relies on stateless communication and is often used for web services. In the case of model deployment, a RESTful API exposes endpoints for making predictions, which can be called by other systems or users.

2.2 Setting Up a Simple API with plumber

Let's go through the basic steps of creating a simple API using the **plumber** package. This API will serve predictions from a trained machine learning model. In this case, let's assume we've built a linear regression model to predict website traffic based on various features (e.g., marketing spend, social media activity).

1. **Install the necessary packages**:

To use **plumber**, you'll first need to install it from CRAN.

r

```
install.packages("plumber")
install.packages("caret")  # for model building and predictions
```

2. **Create an R script for the API**:

In your R script, you will define your model, load the required libraries, and then create endpoints to serve predictions.

r

```r
library(plumber)
library(caret)


# Load your trained model (e.g., linear regression model)
model <- readRDS("website_traffic_model.rds")


# Define the Plumber API


#' @post /predict
#' @param marketing_spend numeric
#' @param social_media_activity numeric
#' @param previous_traffic numeric
#' @return numeric
#' This endpoint predicts website traffic based on input features
function(marketing_spend, social_media_activity,
previous_traffic) {
```

```r
# Create a data frame from the inputs
input_data <- data.frame(
  marketing_spend = as.numeric(marketing_spend),
  social_media_activity = as.numeric(social_media_activity),
  previous_traffic = as.numeric(previous_traffic)
)

# Make a prediction using the model
prediction <- predict(model, input_data)

# Return the prediction as a response
return(list(prediction = prediction))
}

# Start the Plumber API
pr <- plumb("api.R")  # Assuming this script is saved as api.R
pr$run(port = 8000)
```

In this example:

- We define a POST endpoint /predict, which takes in three parameters: marketing_spend, social_media_activity, and previous_traffic.

- The function uses the trained linear regression model (saved as website_traffic_model.rds) to make predictions based on the input features.

- The prediction is returned in a JSON format with the key prediction.

3. **Running the API**:

Once you have defined your R script, you can start the API by running it in your R console. This will start a local server that listens on port 8000 (or any other port you specify). You can then access the API via HTTP requests, such as through a browser or using a tool like curl or Postman.

bash

```
curl -X POST http://localhost:8000/predict \
 -d "marketing_spend=1000&social_media_activity=500&previous_traffic=10000"
```

This request would send the input features to the API and return the predicted website traffic.

2.3 Exposing the API to the Web

While running the Plumber API locally is useful for testing, you will eventually want to deploy it to the web so that other systems or users can access it. To do this, you can deploy the API to a cloud service or hosting platform, such as:

- **ShinyApps.io**: A cloud-based service for hosting R-based applications, including APIs.

- **Amazon Web Services (AWS)**: Using EC2 or Lambda functions to host your API.

- **Docker**: Packaging your API into a Docker container and deploying it to any cloud infrastructure or server.

- **DigitalOcean**: A cloud provider where you can deploy your R APIs on virtual private servers.

For simplicity, we'll focus on ShinyApps.io, which offers an easy-to-use platform for deploying R applications.

- To deploy the API, you would use the rsconnect package, which allows you to deploy R-based apps and APIs to ShinyApps.io.

r

```
install.packages("rsconnect")

library(rsconnect)


# Deploy to ShinyApps.io

rsconnect::deployApp("path_to_your_api_folder")
```

Once deployed, your API will be accessible via a URL provided by ShinyApps.io. You can then use this URL to interact with your model from other applications.

3. Real-World Example: Deploying a Predictive Model to Predict Website Traffic

Let's walk through the example of deploying a predictive model for website traffic. Suppose you've built a linear regression model that predicts website traffic based on marketing spend, social media activity, and previous traffic. The goal is to create an API that takes these three features as input and returns the predicted website traffic.

3.1 Model Building

First, you would build a linear regression model using your dataset. In this case, assume that you have a dataset containing features such as marketing_spend, social_media_activity, and previous_traffic, and the target variable is website_traffic.

r

```r
library(caret)


# Load data (assuming a dataset with relevant features)
data <- read.csv("website_traffic_data.csv")


# Train a linear regression model
```

```
model <- train(website_traffic ~ marketing_spend +
social_media_activity + previous_traffic,

        data = data, method = "lm")
```

```
# Save the model

saveRDS(model, "website_traffic_model.rds")
```

3.2 Creating the API

Once the model is trained and saved, you can use the **plumber** package to expose the model as an API, as shown in the previous section. The /predict endpoint would take input features and return the predicted website traffic.

3.3 Testing the API

Before deploying the model to production, it is essential to test the API locally using tools like curl or Postman. You would test the /predict endpoint by sending different sets of input features and verifying that the model returns the correct predictions.

3.4 Monitoring and Scaling the API

Once your API is live and handling real-time predictions, it's important to monitor its performance and ensure that it can handle increased traffic. This can be done by:

- Using **API rate limiting** to prevent abuse and excessive load.

- Monitoring the API's performance, such as latency and response time.

- Scaling the infrastructure by adding more instances of the API or using serverless architecture to handle demand.

3.5 Continuous Integration and Deployment (CI/CD)

To streamline the process of updating your model and API, you can implement Continuous Integration and Continuous Deployment (CI/CD). This involves automating the process of testing, building, and deploying updates to your model or API. Popular tools for CI/CD include GitHub Actions, Jenkins, and GitLab CI.

In this chapter, we've explored how to deploy machine learning models using R, with a focus on creating APIs with the **plumber** package. We covered the entire workflow from model training to deployment, including:

- Understanding the challenges of model deployment.

- Using **plumber** to create and expose machine learning models as RESTful APIs.

- Deploying the API to the cloud with platforms like ShinyApps.io.

- A real-world example of deploying a website traffic prediction model.

Model deployment is an essential skill for data scientists, as it allows them to take their models from development into production, where they can deliver value to users and businesses

Chapter 17: Working with Big Data in R

Introduction

As the world becomes increasingly data-driven, data scientists and analysts are faced with the challenge of processing and analyzing large volumes of data, often referred to as "big data." Traditional data analysis tools, while effective for small to moderately sized datasets, can struggle when faced with large-scale data. This is where specialized big data tools and frameworks come into play.

In this chapter, we'll explore how to work with big data in R, focusing on two powerful packages: **data.table** and **sparklyr**. These packages allow you to handle and process large datasets efficiently, whether you're working with large local files or distributed computing environments. We'll also walk through a real-world example of analyzing large e-commerce transaction data, where we'll demonstrate the use of **data.table** and **sparklyr** for big data analysis.

---

1. Introduction to Big Data and Distributed Computing in R

1.1 What is Big Data?

Big data refers to datasets that are so large and complex that traditional data processing tools and techniques cannot handle them effectively. The three main characteristics of big data are often described by the **three Vs**:

- **Volume**: The sheer amount of data (e.g., terabytes or petabytes).

- **Velocity**: The speed at which data is generated and must be processed.

- **Variety**: The different types and sources of data, which may include structured, semi-structured, and unstructured data.

Big data is not just about large datasets; it also involves advanced techniques for storage, processing, and analysis. In R, handling big data typically involves optimizing memory usage and parallelizing computation.

1.2 Distributed Computing

Distributed computing refers to the practice of dividing a computational task into smaller sub-tasks, which are processed simultaneously on multiple machines or cores. This can dramatically speed up data processing tasks when dealing with large datasets.

R integrates with distributed computing environments like Apache Spark, Hadoop, and cloud platforms (AWS, Google Cloud) to process big data in parallel. The **sparklyr** package, in particular, allows R users to interface with Apache Spark, a fast and general-purpose cluster-computing system.

In this chapter, we'll focus on two primary tools for big data analysis in R: **data.table** for efficient single-node computation and **sparklyr** for distributed computing.

---

2. Using the data.table Package

2.1 What is data.table?

The **data.table** package is an R package that provides an enhanced version of the data.frame. It is optimized for large datasets, offering high-performance aggregation, indexing, and sorting operations. **data.table** is widely used for big data analysis in R because of its speed, ease of use, and flexibility. It provides:

- **Fast reading and writing** of large datasets.

- **Efficient subsetting and filtering** of data.

- **Aggregation and summarization** using the by keyword.

- **In-memory processing** that reduces the need for multiple copies of the data.

2.2 Creating and Manipulating Data with data.table

To use **data.table**, you need to first install and load the package:

r

```
install.packages("data.table")
```

```
library(data.table)
```

Once the package is loaded, you can create a **data.table** from a **data.frame** or read in a dataset directly from a file.

r

```r
# Create a data.table from a data.frame
df <- data.frame(ID = 1:5, Name = c("Alice", "Bob", "Charlie", "David", "Eva"), Age = c(25, 30, 35, 40, 45))
dt <- as.data.table(df)
```

```r
# Read a large CSV file into a data.table
large_data <- fread("large_data.csv")
```

data.table provides several syntax enhancements over data.frames. For example, you can perform in-place modifications without having to create a new object:

r

```r
# Filter data with data.table
dt[Age > 30]  # Returns rows where Age > 30
```

```r
# Perform aggregation by group
dt[, .(Average_Age = mean(Age)), by = Name]
```

2.3 Performance Considerations with data.table

data.table is optimized for speed and memory efficiency. It uses reference semantics, meaning that modifications to a **data.table** are done in place, which helps avoid unnecessary copies of large datasets. Some important performance optimizations to note are:

- **Efficient indexing**: **data.table** allows for efficient indexing on columns, which speeds up subsetting and joining operations.

- **Optimized sorting and grouping**: **data.table** is faster than the base **data.frame** for sorting and grouping large datasets.

- **Parallel processing**: **data.table** can handle parallel processing by using the **parallel** package or future package for multi-core processing.

For instance, to speed up operations on large datasets, you can use the setkey function to create an index on a column:

r

```
setkey(dt, Name)  # Sets an index on the Name
column
```

Once the data is indexed, operations like joining or subsetting become much faster.

3. Using sparklyr for Distributed Big Data

3.1 What is sparklyr?

sparklyr is an R package that allows R users to interact with Apache Spark, a powerful distributed computing system for big data processing. Apache Spark is capable of handling large datasets across multiple machines and is widely used in big data applications for tasks like ETL (extract, transform, load), machine learning, and data processing.

With **sparklyr**, you can connect to a Spark cluster, manage distributed datasets, and perform computations in parallel across a cluster of machines. This enables R users to scale their computations beyond the limits of a single machine.

3.2 Setting Up Apache Spark with sparklyr

To use **sparklyr**, you need to install and configure the package and Spark. Here's how you can do it:

r

```
# Install the sparklyr package

install.packages("sparklyr")

library(sparklyr)


# Install Spark (if not already installed)
```

```r
spark_install()


# Connect to a local Spark cluster

sc <- spark_connect(master = "local")
```

Once connected to Spark, you can use **sparklyr** to load, manipulate, and analyze large datasets using Spark's distributed processing power. For example, to load a large dataset into Spark:

r

```r
# Load a large dataset into Spark

large_data_spark <- spark_read_csv(sc, "large_data", "large_data.csv")


# Perform operations on the Spark dataset

large_data_spark %>%

  filter(Age > 30) %>%

  group_by(Name) %>%

  summarise(Average_Age = mean(Age)) %>%

  collect()  # Collect results back to R
```

In this example, we load a CSV file into Spark, filter and group the data, and calculate the average age by name. The collect() function retrieves the results from the Spark cluster and brings them back into R for further analysis.

3.3 Scaling and Optimizing with sparklyr

One of the main benefits of using **sparklyr** is that it allows you to scale your computations across multiple machines or cores. If you have access to a Spark cluster, you can use it to process massive datasets in parallel, distributing the workload across multiple machines.

To scale beyond a single machine, you can use the following setup:

r

```
# Connect to a remote Spark cluster

sc <- spark_connect(master = "spark://your_spark_cluster_address")
```

Spark's ability to perform distributed computing allows it to process datasets that are larger than the available memory on a single machine.

3.4 Real-World Example: Analyzing Large E-Commerce Transaction Data

Let's now walk through a real-world example where we use **data.table** and **sparklyr** to analyze large e-commerce transaction data. Imagine we are tasked with analyzing customer transactions from an e-commerce platform, which contains millions of records.

The dataset includes the following columns:

- **Transaction ID**: Unique identifier for each transaction.

- **Customer ID**: Unique identifier for each customer.

- **Product ID**: ID of the purchased product.

- **Quantity**: Number of items purchased.

- **Price**: Price per item.

- **Timestamp**: Date and time of purchase.

Step 1: Loading Data

With data.table:

If the dataset fits into memory, we can use **data.table** to load and process the data:

r

```
library(data.table)

ecommerce_data <- fread("ecommerce_data.csv")
```

With sparklyr:

If the dataset is too large to fit into memory, we can use **sparklyr** to load the data into a Spark cluster:

r

```
library(sparklyr)

sc <- spark_connect(master = "local")

ecommerce_data_spark <- spark_read_csv(sc,
"ecommerce_data", "ecommerce_data.csv")
```

Step 2: Data Cleaning and Transformation

Using **data.table**, we can quickly clean and transform the data:

r

```
# Remove rows with missing values
ecommerce_data <- ecommerce_data[!is.na(Price) & !is.na(Quantity)]

# Calculate total value per transaction
ecommerce_data[, TotalValue := Price * Quantity]
```

With **sparklyr**, the operations are similar but performed on a distributed dataset:

r

```
ecommerce_data_spark %>%
  filter(!is.na(Price) & !is.na(Quantity)) %>%
  mutate(TotalValue = Price * Quantity) %>%
  collect()  # Bring the result back to R
```

Step 3: Aggregation and Insights

Now, let's perform some basic aggregation, such as calculating the total sales by product:

r

```
# With data.table

ecommerce_data[, .(TotalSales = sum(TotalValue)),
by = ProductID]
```

Or with **sparklyr**:

r

```
ecommerce_data_spark %>%

  group_by(ProductID) %>%

  summarise(TotalSales = sum(TotalValue)) %>%

  collect()
```

In this chapter, we explored how to work with big data in R using two powerful tools: **data.table** and **sparklyr**. Both of these tools are optimized for handling large datasets, but they operate in different environments:

- **data.table** is perfect for fast, in-memory processing on a single machine.

- **sparklyr** provides a way to scale your computations across multiple machines using Apache Spark.

We demonstrated how to use these packages to analyze large e-commerce transaction data, covering the entire process from loading data to performing aggregations and calculations. By leveraging **data.table** and **sparklyr**, data scientists and analysts can efficiently analyze big data and extract valuable insights from massive datasets.

Chapter 18: Ethics and Best Practices in Data Science

Introduction

Data science is transforming every aspect of our lives. From healthcare and finance to social media and law enforcement, data-driven algorithms are increasingly influencing the decisions we make. As the power and scope of these technologies grow, so too does the responsibility that comes with them. Ethical considerations in data science are more crucial than ever before, as biased models, privacy violations, and unfair outcomes can have profound real-world consequences.

In this chapter, we will explore the ethical implications of data science, including key topics like data privacy, transparency, and fairness in model building. We will also examine some of the challenges that data scientists face when trying to align their work with ethical guidelines. A real-world example, **predictive policing systems**, will help illustrate these concerns and highlight the importance of ethical decision-making in data science.

1. Understanding the Ethical Implications of Data Science

1.1 The Power and Responsibility of Data Science

At its core, data science is the process of extracting insights from data through analysis, machine learning, and modeling. This can result in powerful outcomes — for example, predicting disease outbreaks, detecting fraudulent transactions, or recommending content that aligns with user interests. However, data science also carries significant risks, particularly when algorithms are applied to areas that directly affect people's lives.

As data science continues to influence sectors like criminal justice, healthcare, hiring, and lending, the need for ethical considerations becomes more pressing. Data scientists are not just tasked with building models that are technically accurate — they must also ensure that their models are fair, transparent, and responsible.

1.2 Ethical Concerns in Data Science

Some of the major ethical concerns that arise in the field of data science include:

- **Bias and Fairness**: Machine learning models, while seemingly objective, can perpetuate or even exacerbate biases inherent in the data. This can lead to unfair outcomes, such as discrimination against certain groups.

- **Data Privacy**: With the increasing amount of personal data being collected, there are concerns about how that data is used, who has access to it, and how it is protected.

- **Transparency**: Many machine learning models, particularly deep learning models, are often described as "black boxes" because their decision-making processes are difficult to interpret. Lack of transparency can lead to mistrust, and even worse, unintended consequences.

- **Accountability**: When decisions are made by algorithms, it is crucial to understand who is responsible for those decisions. If a model makes an error or results in harm, who is held accountable?

2. Data Privacy, Transparency, and Fairness in Model Building

2.1 Data Privacy: Protecting Individuals' Information

As organizations collect more personal data for analysis, data privacy becomes a critical concern. In the context of data science, privacy refers to the protection of personal information from unauthorized access, misuse, or exposure. Many countries have enacted data protection regulations, such as the **General Data Protection Regulation (GDPR)** in the

European Union, which enforces strict rules about how companies handle personal data.

Here are some key principles and best practices related to data privacy in data science:

- **Minimization of Data**: Only collect data that is necessary for the specific analysis or task. Avoid over-collecting data that may increase risks.

- **Anonymization and Pseudonymization**: In some cases, it is possible to anonymize or pseudonymize data to protect individual identities while still being able to perform meaningful analysis.

- **User Consent**: Ensure that individuals are informed about how their data will be used and obtain their explicit consent.

- **Data Security**: Implement robust security measures to protect sensitive data from breaches, including encryption, secure storage, and access controls.

Real-World Example: GDPR in Action

The GDPR has set new standards for how organizations must handle personal data. It mandates that companies must clearly inform users about the data they collect, how it will be used, and who will have access to it. For instance, companies that use personal data for training machine learning models must obtain consent and provide users with the right to access, correct, or delete their data.

2.2 Transparency: Making Models Understandable

Transparency in data science refers to the ability to understand how a model makes its predictions. In many domains, particularly in high-stakes decision-making (such as healthcare or criminal justice), the decisions made by algorithms can have serious consequences. Lack of transparency can lead to a loss of trust and the potential for misuse.

Challenges in Achieving Transparency:

- **Black Box Models**: Machine learning models, especially deep learning algorithms, often operate as "black boxes," meaning their internal workings are not easily interpretable by humans.

- **Complexity of Algorithms**: As models become more sophisticated, they may involve layers of decisions that are difficult for even experts to fully understand.

Best Practices for Transparency:

- **Explainable AI**: Researchers and practitioners are increasingly focused on building explainable AI systems. Tools like **LIME** (Local Interpretable Model-agnostic Explanations) and **SHAP** (SHapley Additive exPlanations) are being used to interpret and explain complex models.

- **Documentation**: Keep thorough documentation of the models used, including assumptions made, the training data used, and the steps taken to develop the model. This provides a record that can be audited.

- **Communication**: When deploying models, especially in sensitive areas, it is important to communicate how decisions are made to the stakeholders, including users, customers, and affected parties.

2.3 Fairness: Ensuring Equal Treatment

Fairness in data science refers to ensuring that models do not disproportionately disadvantage any particular group. Algorithms can unintentionally perpetuate biases present in historical data, leading to unfair outcomes. For example, a hiring algorithm trained on historical hiring data might inadvertently favor candidates from certain demographics while disadvantaging others.

There are different approaches to ensuring fairness in machine learning:

- **Bias Detection**: Use techniques to detect and mitigate bias in training data. This can involve auditing the data for disproportionate representation of certain groups and removing or balancing out biases.

- **Fairness Constraints**: When building models, incorporate fairness constraints that ensure that the predictions do not differ unfairly between groups (e.g., gender, race, or socioeconomic status).

- **Post-Processing**: After a model is trained, adjustments can be made to the model's predictions to make them more equitable.

Real-World Example: Predictive Policing Systems

Predictive policing refers to the use of algorithms to forecast where crimes are likely to occur or who is more likely to commit a crime. These systems typically use historical crime data to train predictive models. However, predictive policing has been widely criticized for reinforcing biases in policing.

For example, if historical crime data reflects systemic biases in law enforcement practices (e.g., disproportionately policing certain neighborhoods or demographics), then predictive models trained on that data may continue to target those same neighborhoods or demographics, leading to a vicious cycle of over-policing.

Ethical challenges arise in such systems because they risk reinforcing societal biases, leading to unfair and discriminatory outcomes. The fairness of predictive policing models has been called into question due to their potential to perpetuate racial and socio-economic disparities.

Steps to Address Fairness:

- **Bias Audits**: Regularly audit the data used in predictive policing systems for bias and make adjustments to ensure the model does not unfairly target certain groups.

- **Transparency in Decision-Making**: Provide clear and accessible information about how predictions are made and what data is being used to make those predictions.

- **Accountability**: Ensure that police departments and organizations using predictive policing systems are held accountable for the outcomes of these models, and establish mechanisms for affected communities to challenge or appeal decisions.

---

3. Best Practices in Ethical Data Science

To avoid ethical pitfalls in data science, it is crucial to follow a set of best practices. These practices help ensure that data science is performed responsibly, transparently, and with fairness in mind.

3.1 Responsible Data Collection

- **Use ethically sourced data**: Ensure that the data used for training models is obtained ethically, with consent from individuals when required.

- **Data minimization**: Collect only the data that is necessary for your analysis or model-building process. This reduces the risk of privacy violations and helps ensure the data is not misused.

3.2 Fairness by Design

- **Incorporate fairness from the start**: Fairness should not be an afterthought but integrated into the design of models and processes.

- **Use fairness metrics**: Monitor the fairness of models using fairness metrics, such as demographic parity, equal opportunity, and fairness through awareness.

- **Test for discrimination**: Regularly test your models to ensure they are not discriminating against certain groups.

3.3 Transparency and Explainability

- **Model explainability**: Strive for model explainability, especially in high-stakes situations like healthcare or criminal justice.

- **Clear communication**: Clearly communicate how models make decisions and the factors that influence these decisions.

- **Documentation and auditing**: Keep detailed records of the modeling process, including the assumptions made, the datasets used, and the ethical considerations taken into account.

3.4 Accountability

- **Be accountable for outcomes**: If a model produces an unfair or harmful outcome, it is the responsibility of the data scientists and organizations involved to address and correct it.

- **Establish accountability frameworks**: Create mechanisms for the oversight and accountability of algorithms, especially when they are used in critical areas like policing, hiring, and healthcare.

Data science has the potential to solve complex problems and create innovative solutions. However, with this power comes significant responsibility. As data scientists, we must be conscious of the ethical implications of our work, ensuring that our models are fair, transparent, and respect privacy. By adhering to best practices and actively working to mitigate biases and ethical risks, we can ensure that data science continues to be a force for good, making meaningful contributions to society.

Chapter 19: Advanced Topics and Future Trends in Data Science and R

Introduction

As the world becomes more data-driven, the field of data science continues to evolve at an exponential rate. New technologies, algorithms, and methodologies are emerging at a pace that can sometimes feel overwhelming. One of the most promising tools for staying on top of these trends is R, a programming language that has been a cornerstone in data science for over two decades. With its rich ecosystem of packages and strong community support, R continues to be at the forefront of developing new techniques for data analysis, machine learning, and artificial intelligence (AI).

In this chapter, we will explore the **advanced topics** in data science, focusing on **cutting-edge AI and machine learning algorithms**, as well as the **future of R in data science and machine learning**. We will also take a look at some **real-world examples**, particularly in specialized fields such as genomics, where R is already playing a significant role in advancing scientific research.

By the end of this chapter, you will have a deeper understanding of the next frontier in data science, and how you can leverage R to remain competitive in an ever-changing landscape.

---

1. Advancements in AI and Machine Learning Algorithms

1.1 Deep Learning and Neural Networks

One of the most significant advancements in AI and machine learning has been the rise of deep learning. Deep learning is a subset of machine learning that deals with algorithms inspired by the structure and function of the brain, known as neural networks. These models have revolutionized areas such as image recognition, natural language processing, and speech recognition.

Deep learning algorithms are particularly well-suited to handle complex, high-dimensional data like images, audio, and text. Some of the most popular architectures include:

- **Convolutional Neural Networks (CNNs)**: Used primarily in image classification and computer vision tasks.

- **Recurrent Neural Networks (RNNs)**: Well-suited for sequential data, such as time series or natural language.

- **Transformers**: The architecture behind models like GPT (the model you're interacting with) that excels in processing sequential data and is now the foundation for many language models.

In R, the **keras** package, which acts as an R interface to Google's TensorFlow, allows users to easily build, train, and deploy deep learning models. **TensorFlow** and **PyTorch** also have R interfaces, allowing practitioners to take advantage of these powerful libraries while using R as their primary tool.

1.2 Reinforcement Learning (RL)

Another exciting development in AI is **reinforcement learning (RL)**, which focuses on training agents to make a series of decisions by interacting with an environment. Unlike supervised learning, where models are trained on labeled data, reinforcement learning involves learning through trial and error, often by receiving rewards or penalties for actions taken.

The RL paradigm has been used in areas such as robotics, gaming (e.g., AlphaGo), and autonomous vehicles. The **reinforce** package in R allows users to experiment with reinforcement learning algorithms. Researchers are also using RL to optimize everything from supply chain logistics to marketing strategies.

1.3 Transfer Learning

Transfer learning refers to the technique of taking a model trained on one task and repurposing it for another, related task. This is particularly useful when there is a limited amount of data available for the second task. Instead of training a model from scratch, the weights and architecture learned in the first task can be fine-tuned to perform well on the second task.

For example, a neural network trained on a large dataset of images can be used to analyze medical images with relatively small datasets, improving both performance and training efficiency. Transfer learning has become a game-changer in domains where labeled data is scarce.

In R, **tensorflow** and **keras** support transfer learning, providing access to pre-trained models that can be fine-tuned for specific tasks.

1.4 Generative Models and GANs

Generative models, particularly **Generative Adversarial Networks (GANs)**, have seen significant advancements in the AI community. GANs consist of two neural networks — a **generator** and a **discriminator** — that are trained simultaneously. The generator creates synthetic data, and the discriminator evaluates how realistic the data is. Over time, this process results in the generator producing highly realistic data.

GANs are used in a variety of applications, from generating photorealistic images to creating music and videos. In R, researchers are increasingly adopting **tensorflow** and **keras** for building GANs.

2. The Future of R in Data Science and Machine Learning

R has long been considered one of the most powerful tools for data science, thanks to its extensive package ecosystem and ease of use for statistical analysis. But what about the future of R? How will it continue to evolve in the face of growing competition from languages like Python, which has a dominant presence in machine learning and AI?

2.1 R's Integration with AI and Deep Learning

While Python may have the upper hand in some areas of AI development, R is quickly catching up, especially when it comes to integrating deep learning and machine learning. With the introduction of packages like **keras**, **tensorflow**, and **mxnet**, R users can now leverage some of the most advanced AI tools available.

In particular, R's strength in data wrangling and visualization (with packages like **dplyr** and **ggplot2**) makes it an excellent choice for data preprocessing and model interpretation. This gives R a unique advantage in the AI ecosystem, where a model's interpretability and understanding of data are often just as important as its predictive power.

2.2 R's Role in Big Data and Distributed Computing

As the size of datasets grows, so does the need for distributed computing and big data tools. R is making strides in this area, with packages like **sparklyr** (for integrating R with Apache Spark) and **data.table** (for in-memory data manipulation). These tools allow R users to work with massive datasets that would be impossible to handle on a single machine.

Furthermore, R is increasingly being integrated with cloud-based tools and platforms like **Amazon Web Services (AWS)**, **Google Cloud**, and **Microsoft Azure**, making it easier for users to scale their computations and deploy models in the cloud.

2.3 R in the Internet of Things (IoT)

With the rise of IoT devices that generate huge volumes of data, there is a growing need to analyze this data in real-time. R's capabilities in time series analysis and its integration with real-time data streams position it as a powerful tool for IoT analytics.

Packages like **shiny** and **plumber** are being used to create web applications that can handle IoT data in real-time, allowing users to monitor and respond to events as they happen.

2.4 Enhancements in Model Interpretability and Explainability

As AI models become more complex, understanding how they make decisions becomes crucial. In high-stakes applications like healthcare and criminal justice, model transparency is a must.

R is actively involved in the development of tools to improve model interpretability. **LIME** (Local Interpretable Model-Agnostic Explanations) and **SHAP** (SHapley Additive exPlanations) are both available in R, allowing data scientists to understand how machine learning models arrive at their predictions.

As AI systems continue to affect people's lives, model transparency and fairness will become central issues. R's active community in these areas suggests that the language will play an important role in ensuring the responsible deployment of machine learning models.

3. Real-World Example: R in Genomics

One of the most exciting and impactful applications of R is in **genomics**, where it is helping researchers understand complex biological processes, develop personalized treatments, and discover new drugs.

3.1 Genomic Data Analysis with R

Genomics involves the study of an organism's genome, which contains all of its genetic material. The sheer size and complexity of genomic data present significant challenges for data scientists. Fortunately, R has a number of packages specifically designed for the analysis of genomic data. Some of the key packages include:

- **Bioconductor**: A collection of R packages for the analysis and comprehension of high-throughput genomic data.

- **edgeR** and **DESeq2**: Used for differential gene expression analysis.

- **GenomicRanges**: For manipulating genomic data.

3.2 Genomic Data Visualization

Visualizing genomic data is a key part of the process, and R excels in this area. Researchers use **ggplot2** and other visualization tools to create plots and heatmaps that help identify patterns in gene expression, mutations, and other genetic factors.

In particular, the ability to visualize genetic data in conjunction with clinical data is helping to improve personalized medicine and drug discovery. For example, using **ggplot2**, researchers can visualize how specific genes correlate with certain types of cancers, enabling more targeted treatments.

3.3 Personalized Medicine and Drug Discovery

R is also making an impact in **personalized medicine** and **drug discovery**. By analyzing genomic data, clinical data, and patient histories, data scientists can help doctors design customized treatment plans based on a person's unique genetic makeup. R has played a pivotal role in analyzing the vast amount of data generated by high-throughput sequencing and other genomic technologies, making it an essential tool in the field of precision medicine.

Real-World Example: Cancer Genomics

In cancer genomics, R is used to analyze data from tumor samples to identify mutations and understand how they drive cancer progression. Tools like **Bioconductor** allow researchers to integrate different types of genomic data, such as RNA sequencing and

DNA methylation data, to gain insights into cancer biology.

By identifying biomarkers specific to different types of cancer, researchers can develop personalized therapies that target these biomarkers. This approach has the potential to revolutionize cancer treatment by enabling more effective and less toxic therapies.

The world of data science is constantly evolving, with new algorithms, tools, and techniques emerging on a regular basis. R, with its rich ecosystem of packages and strong community support, continues to be at the forefront of these advancements. From deep learning to reinforcement learning, transfer learning, and GANs, R is helping data scientists stay on top of cutting-edge developments in AI and machine learning.

The future of R in data science looks bright, especially with its increasing integration with big data, cloud computing, and real-time analytics. As the language evolves, R will continue to play a central role in helping organizations solve some of the most complex problems in fields like genomics, healthcare, and beyond.

Conclusion: The Future of Data Science and R

As we've seen throughout this book, R has long been a powerful tool for data science, machine learning, and statistical analysis. Its flexibility, rich ecosystem, and deep integration with cutting-edge technologies have cemented its position as one of the most widely used programming languages in the world. Whether you are an aspiring data scientist, a researcher in academia, or a professional in the industry, mastering R can open doors to incredible opportunities in fields ranging from business analytics to healthcare, finance, and beyond.

In this final chapter, we'll reflect on the journey we've taken together through the world of data science and R. We'll highlight the key concepts and techniques that we've covered and discuss how you can continue to build on this knowledge as you embark on your own data science journey. Moreover, we'll explore the future of R in data science and machine learning, and how you can leverage its growing ecosystem to stay ahead in this fast-paced and ever-evolving field.

Recap of Key Concepts and Skills

Throughout the chapters of this book, we've built a solid foundation in using R for data analysis, visualization, and machine learning. Here's a quick recap of some of the most important concepts and skills you've learned:

1. Introduction to R and RStudio

- We started by exploring the fundamentals of R programming, setting up R and RStudio, and familiarizing ourselves with the basic syntax.

- The RStudio interface was introduced as an essential tool for coding, visualizing, and debugging R scripts.

- We also learned about the power of packages in R, such as ggplot2, dplyr, and caret, and how they are used to manipulate and visualize data.

2. Data Types and Structures in R

- A deep understanding of data types, such as numeric, character, and logical, and structures like vectors, matrices, data frames, and lists helped us understand how to organize and manipulate data effectively.

- We focused on how to work with real-world datasets like customer data, building data frames and performing basic manipulations.

3. Data Cleaning and Preprocessing

- We delved into the crucial aspects of data cleaning, addressing missing values, outliers, and ensuring that the data was in a usable format for analysis.

- Transformations like scaling and normalization were introduced, showing how data preprocessing is key to building accurate machine learning models.

4. Data Manipulation with dplyr and tidyr

- The dplyr and tidyr packages were explored in-depth for their powerful capabilities in data manipulation.

- Through real-world examples like employee performance data analysis, we saw how filtering, grouping, and summarizing data could reveal valuable insights.

5. Exploratory Data Analysis (EDA)

- We discussed the importance of EDA in data science: understanding the data, its distributions, and relationships among variables before moving forward with complex models.

- We used visualizations, such as histograms and scatter plots, to explore online retail sales data.

6. Data Visualization with ggplot2

- The ggplot2 package was covered extensively as a means to create aesthetically pleasing and informative visualizations.

- We explored various types of plots, from simple bar charts to more complex scatter plots and line charts, including how to customize them for better storytelling.

7. Statistical Models in R

- Linear regression and logistic regression were covered as foundational models for predictive analysis.

- Real-world applications, such as predicting house prices and classifying outcomes with logistic regression, demonstrated how to apply these models to solve real problems.

8. Building Classification Models

- Classification models such as decision trees and k-nearest neighbors (k-NN) were introduced to tackle problems where the output is categorical.

- We worked on predicting customer churn, one of the most practical applications of classification in business.

9. Regression Models for Predictive Analytics

- We deepened our understanding of regression analysis, both linear and polynomial, for predictive analytics.

- Real-world examples, like forecasting sales for a retail business, demonstrated how regression models could be applied to predict future trends.

10. Machine Learning with Random Forests and SVM

- The caret package in R was utilized to implement Random Forests and Support Vector Machines (SVM) for complex predictive modeling.

- By predicting loan defaults using Random Forests, we saw the power of ensemble methods and the importance of hyperparameter tuning.

11. Neural Networks and Deep Learning with R

- Neural networks and deep learning concepts were introduced using the keras package, bridging the gap between R and TensorFlow.

- We built a basic neural network for image classification, demonstrating how deep learning could be applied to cutting-edge tasks.

12. Model Evaluation and Hyperparameter Tuning

- We learned how to assess model performance using metrics like RMSE and R-squared, and explored techniques like cross-validation and confusion matrices.

- Hyperparameter tuning via grid search allowed us to fine-tune classification models, such as email spam detection, to achieve better performance.

13. Time Series Forecasting with R

- Time series forecasting techniques such as ARIMA, Exponential Smoothing, and Prophet were discussed.

- By forecasting demand for a product over time, we saw the value of time series analysis in making data-driven decisions.

14. Clustering and Unsupervised Learning

- K-means clustering and hierarchical clustering techniques were used for grouping data into meaningful clusters.

- We worked through a real-world example of customer segmentation based on purchase behavior, which is vital for targeted marketing strategies.

15. Natural Language Processing (NLP) in R

- The basics of NLP, text mining, and sentiment analysis were introduced, with R libraries like tm and tidytext.

- We analyzed social media posts to detect brand sentiment, demonstrating how text data can be mined for valuable insights.

16. Model Deployment and APIs with R

- The process of deploying models into production environments was covered, using the plumber package to create APIs.

- By deploying a predictive model for website traffic, we saw how data science models can be made accessible to end-users via web interfaces.

17. Working with Big Data in R

- Big data tools like data.table and sparklyr were explored, allowing R to handle large datasets efficiently.

- We looked at how to process and analyze large e-commerce transaction data, providing insights for businesses operating at scale.

18. Ethics and Best Practices in Data Science

- Ethical considerations in data science, such as data privacy, fairness, and model transparency, were emphasized.

- By analyzing predictive policing systems, we saw how data science can be misused if ethical concerns are ignored.

19. Advanced Topics and Future Trends in Data Science and R

- We explored the future of data science, including advancements in AI, machine learning algorithms, and deep learning, and how R is positioned to lead in these areas.

- From genomics to precision medicine, R's role in shaping the future of specialized fields was highlighted.

The Future of Data Science: An Evolving Landscape

Data science and machine learning are evolving rapidly, with new algorithms, techniques, and tools emerging regularly. The pace of innovation in AI, deep learning, and machine learning means that data science professionals must continuously learn and adapt to stay relevant. R, however, remains a powerful and adaptable tool that continues to evolve along with the field.

As we've seen throughout this book, R is not just a tool for simple statistical analysis but has become an integral part of the modern data science toolkit. From machine learning and deep learning to big data analysis and natural language processing, R's flexibility and ease of use make it a top choice for practitioners in many fields.

The future of R lies in its increasing integration with big data tools, cloud platforms, and advanced AI frameworks. Its ability to seamlessly interface with powerful libraries like TensorFlow and PyTorch will continue to drive its relevance in deep learning, while the ongoing development of packages like sparklyr ensures that it remains competitive in the big data space.

Additionally, as data science becomes more interdisciplinary, R's use in specialized fields like genomics, healthcare, and personalized medicine will only grow. With its robust statistical capabilities and the strength of the **Bioconductor** ecosystem, R is poised to play a critical role in advancing scientific discovery and technological innovation.

Moving Forward: Building Your Data Science Journey

Now that you have a comprehensive understanding of R for data science and machine learning, the next step is to apply your knowledge to real-world problems. Here are a few recommendations on how to proceed:

1. Experiment with Real-World Datasets

- Begin by working with publicly available datasets from sources like Kaggle, UCI Machine Learning Repository, and government open data portals. The more you practice, the better your skills will become.

- Try applying the various machine learning models and techniques you've learned throughout this book to gain hands-on experience. The best way to learn is by doing.

2. Contribute to Open-Source Projects

- Consider contributing to open-source data science projects on platforms like GitHub. This will help you build a portfolio, work with other data scientists, and get feedback on your work.

- By contributing to projects that use R, you can deepen your understanding of the language and the data science field.

3. Stay Updated on New Developments

- The field of data science is always evolving. Subscribe to newsletters, join relevant forums, and participate in data science communities to keep up with the latest developments.

- Attend data science and machine learning conferences, webinars, and meetups to network with professionals and stay informed about cutting-edge advancements.

4. Pursue Specialized Learning Paths

- R has specific libraries and tools tailored to different domains, such as bioinformatics, finance, and economics. Consider exploring these fields in more depth to gain specialized knowledge.

- You may also wish to study more advanced topics in AI and machine learning, such as reinforcement learning, neural architecture search, or explainable AI.

Final Thoughts: The Power of Data Science

The journey you've undertaken through the world of data science with R is just the beginning. The tools and techniques you've learned will serve as the foundation upon which you can continue to build. Data science has the power to transform industries, solve complex societal challenges, and provide deep insights into the world around us.

As you continue your journey, remember that learning is a continuous process. Data science is not just about mastering algorithms or statistical techniques—it's about solving problems, thinking critically, and adapting to an ever-changing landscape. The more you engage with data, the more you'll uncover new opportunities and potential.

Ultimately, whether you're working on predictive models, exploring big data, or building AI systems, remember the key to success is curiosity and persistence. The future of data science is bright, and with R, you are well-equipped to shape that future.